SATURDAY ALWAYS COMES

The Relaxed Way to Sales Success

by
Irwin Burt Meisel, CLU

Victor
Sal On
Burt

FARNSWORTH PUBLISHING COMPANY
a subsidiary of Longman Financial Services Publishing, Inc.
500 North Dearborn Street
Chicago, Illinois 60610-4975

I dedicate this book to my daughter, Shelley, who, at the time of writing, is a rookie agent with tenure of one and a half months in the insurance business. I have lived with Shelley for 23 years and one of her great attributes is dedication to people. In my estimation, there could never have been a more appropriate profession for her than the one known as life insurance sales.

I write books on the subject of simplifying complex ideas so that they are understandable and meaningful to the prospective client. In the last few months, it has been my joy to personally supervise the implementation, knowledge, and study of our products for Shelley. They appear particularly vital when I see my daughter going forth with honesty, enthusiasm, eagerness, and a desire to serve the public. I am as proud as I can be to see her dedication to her prospects and clients. She will do well and will create thousands of beneficiaries but at this moment, the two chief beneficiaries are my wife, Sharon, and I.

The trials and labors of the business have always been worth the battles but when I see the torch passed and lit even brighter, I am exalted and rededicate myself. Sale on, Shelley.

Published by FARNSWORTH PUBLISHING COMPANY
a subsidiary of Longman Financial Services Publishing, Inc.
500 North Dearborn Street
Chicago, Illinois 60610-4975

86   87   88   10   9   8   7   6   5   4   3   2

Library of Congress Catalog Card No. 84-81056.
ISBN 0-87863-222-0.
Manufactured in the United States of America.

cover design: Jeanette Forman

CONTENTS

INTRODUCTION

SATURDAY ALWAYS COMES

The business of selling life insurance is tormenting. The highs and the lows are turbulent. We salespeople constantly talk to each other and to ourselves, searching for the reasons why this discipline known as "selling" can't be tamed to a point of smoothness. Our good days are pure heaven and our bad days are pure, high-grade torture. On the days when we make the satisfying sales, we amuse ourselves with the thought that, "This ain't so tough." We take the day's earnings and multiply it out for a whole year's work, and we say to ourselves, "I'm working at a pretty high rate of pay." I've done that exercise and, on some occasions, I've been the highest income earner the world has ever known. I think that all of us have taken this kind of mathematical placebo. It's simple. The formula is: Take today's commissions times the number of days you work in a year. For those among us who had difficulty solving story problems in high school math, this isn't even that complicated; it's a pure straight calculation: this times that. On the other hand, in the depths of the blank days, the calculations are even simpler: zero times any number is still zero. On those days we're all equal. The biggest of the big become the smallest of the small, and for the briefest tick of time, the newest rookie stands on the same level with the Toppest of the Top of the Table.

Without some kind of safety valve relief, this kind of quick freeze to thaw can cause great physical and mental harm. And it does. That's why we band together like herds of cattle in a blizzard. We need the consolation of other knowing and understanding commiserators. Relief comes in many forms of diversion: sleep, physical exercise, hobbies, vacations, charity and civic work, playing with the kids, church and synagogue, household chores, do-it-yourself projects . . . and Saturday. When I refer to Saturday, I mean two things: both the day itself, and all the other times off the firing line. Saturday always comes.

For the purists and exactists, I must yield to your immediate objection that it doesn't always come. There is an exception to every rule and every fixed idea, so I agree that at least one time, for each of us, Saturday won't come. Therefore, the important point for all of us is: What do we do with all the Saturdays that do come?

I work Saturdays. I always have and I love it. It's a different kind of work. The pressure is off. The staff is off. But the thinking process is on. In our building, we get a Saturday mail delivery, so I am able to open it if I feel like it and get a headstart on the week. It's the time I use to "get my head on straight." All those things that I promise myself I will do later, get done on Saturday. Calculations, dictation, organization of the coming week, a few phone calls, and a lot of thinking get done on that day. The really unique thing is that I am under no compulsion to do any of it. It really can wait and get done in the course of the next regular workweek, but that's what makes it fun. I don't have to do it. I can breeze and not squeeze. The result is that most often more gets done while I'm working at a leisurely pace than gets done when I'm pressing. One of the laws Murphy should incorporate is, "A Saturday hour equals four weekday hours." The phone rings infrequently, I'm unshaven and dressed in anything other than the week's uniform, and I'm enjoying every slow minute of it.

I usually start this routine at 7AM and work to 11AM. Then I leave and go to my club where I play racquetball and clean up. This has been my routine for years. It works, so I don't tamper with success. I'm reminded of the pension client I have who, on the first interview, told me that the cost of the plan was too great. I said, "That's no problem; eliminate the first name. That is where the highest cost comes." He protested, "But that's my name." I responded, "So what? You always told me this wasn't work anyway because you enjoy it so much. So you will probably never retire and there is no use in putting money aside for what will never occur."

His feelings about his work exactly coincide with mine, doubly so on Saturdays. Now, Saturday doesn't always have to come on Saturday; for different people, it can come at different times. The point is that we all have to have some time when there is no pressure so that we can prepare ourselves for the times when there is pressure and we're under the gun to perform. We all need our "down time" just as our computers demand theirs. When that monster is off, nothing else goes on. All of us should be so kind to ourselves. Life ain't easy; business ain't easy. The problems come no matter how carefully we run our affairs and no matter how many "administrative assistants" we have to insulate us from the financial wars. Some guys can go at a meteoric pace continually. Some only do it until the anxiety attacks and stomach pains say that "Man does not live by commissions alone."

My purpose in life is to bring a little bit of Saturday into every day. Life is only so long. None of us has to look very far to see associates with ulcers or heart problems, kids taking narcotics, divorce, financial problems caused by too much social climbing, daily therapy counseling, and stress above and beyond the call of necessity. To cure most of these, nothing will do other than quality time. Money will not do it; in fact, chasing money to ease these problems can frequently accelerate the symptoms. I really, honestly, work to pace myself down and I urge everyone to DO LESS . . . at the right time. This means doing *more* at the right time. Your built-in computer (which is your stomach and not your brain) will tell you when you have an overload or an underload.

The key is balance. When the swings are too far, the problems start. This is where a conscious effort to get off-stage is necessary. This is where we must all try to give the body parts a rest. And this is where Saturday becomes important to me. I'm in the environment I like, but I'm doing it in a relaxing fashion. Accordingly, I started writing this book on a Saturday and I aimed it at a Saturday purpose: to make light about our business, which is often too serious. We'll explore two aspects of the insurance life: the simple side to the complex subject, and the lighthearted approach to the somber profession. We'll poke some fun at ourselves, our clients, and our home offices. We'll take the mystery out of the legalese and the depth of our language and paper output. We'll talk about the nightmares out there in the insurance arena and how, with only a little effort, one can turn them into "daymares" too. We can all be equal-opportunity worriers. There is no discrimination in problems if we let them get the best of us. So with an up-to-date version of the ancient saying, "This too shall pass," I prod you forward into the book with the promise that "Saturday Always Comes."

*   *   *

1.

SIMPLE SIMON SAYS

Simon Says, "Take two giant steps forward." And everyone does. "Take one step backward." And some do. Baby steps, giant steps, forward, backward, up and down—these are some of the simplest instructions or the severest traps if you don't do them right. Some salespeople do take these steps in the wrong direction at the wrong time. Some want to go straight up and scatter, or so it would seem from the hectic scurrying, twists, and turns by which some of us run our jobs, businesses, professions, or practices, depending on one's own view of the calling.

It's a job if it's not going so well. It's a business if we can truly believe we're working for ourselves and will be rewarded according to the efforts we expend, even if it is not happening yet. It's a profession when it's run on a smooth, structured basis, with cause and effect known and expected, either by a solo practitioner, or by a finely tuned, multiperson entity. And it's a "practice" when all of the above pertain, and it's self-perpetuating by proper work habits and motivation.

The object of the kid's game, Simon Says, is entrapment, pure and simple. The leader gives instructions with or
without the words "Simon Says." The leader can use any
means of deception he chooses. He can raise or lower his
voice. He can stall. He can be as elaborate or as cute as he
likes. But the object is single-purposed: create a bunch of
losers and one winner. If he uses the phrase, "Simon says,"
the players obey. If he does not use the phrase, no action is
the right action. The losers self-destruct.

This is only a kid's game, but we have all done it, or are
continually doing it, to ourselves. None of us is immune, but
the difference is that when we apply it to the goal of earning a
living, we can no longer say, "So what?" It is for real when
we take upon ourselves the task of making our own livelihood
by working or by promising to provide other people's liveli-
hoods later on. Life is full of pitfalls, however. Not everyone
can do what everyone else can, but if a person is doing the
"best" he or she can do with what he or she has got, there is
no room for improvement.

I've taken the title of this chapter from the kid's game,
Simon Says, and the nursery rhyme, "Simple Simon." Both
are simple and pure in their intent, and I will try to relate this
childlike logic to my form of selling: simple and pure. Along
with the four aspects of selling I gave above, I should have included the aspect of "game," for selling, in addition to its
serious sides, has all the elements of a game. So I now refer to
the fact that intertwined with the competitive, goal-oriented
nature of the selling business are all the complicated in-
veiglements for this thing innocuously defined as a game.

As salespeople, we've been both praised and criticized by
clients for having told them both "too much" and "too little." We have had people say, "You never told me that."
Also, we've had people say, "Skip all the details, just tell me
what you think I should do." On occasion, both viewpoints
are correct. It is our job to measure what form of presenta-

tion is the proper one for all the circumstances of the meeting. Overkill can be as bad as underinforming the client.

As novices in the business, we are given prepared talks, also known as "canned, boiler-plate, track to run on, memorized, stereotype, cues, spiels, stories, verbatim presentations, exhibits, reports," etc. My feeling is that they are absolutely necessary when taught. Where would an agent be without something to say, and what would he or she say without some form of guidance? Can you imagine the fight the old-time agents must have had, if the stories are true, when they were handed a ratebook and applications, and pushed out the door? In order to start somewhere, we must have something to say or something to show, otherwise there is no communication. So until a salesperson develops his or her own format, the guided path is most likely the right one. This doesn't mean that one can't take the order until every word or every slide is shown, but the well-worn road must have gotten that way for a reason. One old insurance story concerns the agent who wouldn't write the order when asked to because "the client hasn't heard the whole story." Well, to my mind, "the whole story" is just enough to get the job done.

One of life's funny cycles is from formal memorized presentations to free-swinging mental sparring to "my way." What's the definition of "my way"? It's the little personal secure/insecure methods that we all have of doing our own business—"secure" to those on the outside looking in, and "insecure" to ourselves wondering how we can improve and what we are *not* doing that the really big guys *are* doing. "My way" is a mystery to everyone else but the individual whose method it is. It is the reason that industry speakers are eagerly sought out: to impart honestly and openly how they do it.

When these individuals tell how they conduct a meeting, it is usually on a rigid, structured basis. Truly, they developed it themselves after much trial and error, success and failure, highs and lows, and fear and security. I've made many of

these speeches. Before each one, I have momentary doubts
about blatantly telling others, "This is how I do it." First off,
I am continually trying to improve, so I have all the frights of
change. Secondly, when making a speech or writing an article, I must bare my soul and share my qualms, fears, and insecurities. But when the event is over and it was successful, I
realize two things: my audience is also trying to improve, and
my teaching was valuable as a tool to use, or maybe even
more valuable to some listeners as a clear sign of what *not* to
do; and every person in the crowd is sharing with me the same
qualms, fears, and insecurities that I have. But when we come
to this zenith that Frank Sullivan, CLU, labeled "mature
simplicity," what have we done but invented our own
"canned talk"? We're right back where we started, but we
reinvented the wheel and feel good about it because we re-
lived the birth of an idea.

As a result, the sales life cycle is constantly changing in
order to remain the "same." I have paid my good money and
spent my good time attending many, many speakers' meetings just to hear "his way." If "his way" or "my way" is
successful and zeroes in on the points that are presented, it is
without a doubt a memorized presentation. This doesn't necessarily mean that every word and movement is committed to
memory, but the ideas are first nature to the salesperson, and
the care and comfort of all the "my ways" and "his ways"
are the refinement and the tolerance allowance.

If those among us who would swear that we don't have a
defined pattern of interviews would be asked to give a speech
or conduct an interview, we would make an amazing discov-
ery. As we sit down to write the talk and ask ourselves, "How
do I do it?" the measured answer that must come out for a
limited, allotted time in the spotlight would be our own
"canned talk."

We all like to think we are different from everyone else.
The kids have coined the phrase, "Do your own thing." The

thought is a good one: be yourself. But it is tough to be yourself. To prove it, let's go back to the kids. When our generation is far enough removed to be called "history," it will most likely be known as the "Denim Dynasty." The youngsters wanted to be different from their parents. So many wanted to be different that an amazing thing happened: they all started to look alike. The denim look became a uniform and, just like soldiers, no one dared to be caught out of uniform. Then another phenomenon occurred. The older generation, always wanting to look younger, started to wear the denims. Not only did they start wearing them, they wanted to suffer to have them. Enter the designers! They satisfied the style cultists' lust for bloodletting, and the prices soared. And in the eyes of the canvas god, "It was good"; so the prices rose even higher if the clothes were "prewashed." Then it was declared even better when the designers' labels were affixed thereon.

Now, the state of the art has come to precious metals and gems for what used to be called overalls. When they were just overalls, they were left for the laborer and the price was about $10. When they came into vogue and were relabeled "jeans," the price went up to $30. Then they came to the designer's cutting table and the price skyrocketed to three figures. Now with the label being stitched in gold or the rivets and buttons being done in diamonds, the price has climbed to $6,000, and up.

So everyone walks around with someone else's name plastered across his or her derriere. Thus, the development of the "canned" speech. It, too, started out to be different.

In this quest for the "successful" interview, some of us confuse it with the "easy" interview. There is always a price to be paid. If the approach or the first interview is a difficult one, then subsequent interviews or delivery of policies should be smoother. The adage, "There is no such thing as a free lunch," is correct. Sometimes a case comes on a platter, such as an attorney's or accountant's recommendation, where the insurance is presold to a client we haven't even met yet. In these cases, I always proceed cautiously and with an open mind, waiting for the signal when I have to start the selling, even though it was "presold." Invariably, the client comes up with a strong objection that basically boils down to, "That was never explained to me," which when interpreted means, "Tell me more, so that I can get more confidence in you, Mr. Agent," or reinterprets to, "Show me that you know something. I'm not paying all these dollars without getting value."

The message I want to convey by the previous references to prepared presentations, simplified proposals, and "easy" sales is, simply stated, that there is no such thing as an easy sale. I realize immediately that almost every reader's computer will kick in with the memory of a sale that went as smoothly as possible and was a pleasant reward for all the tough ones that we face regularly. I point out that the "easy" one was only the bright spot in the law of averages working for the agent who is doing sufficient numbers of appointments. If the young agent spends all of his time looking for this "easy" sale, or listening to all the propaganda spread by some more experienced agents on "how I do it, kid," he's doomed. There is no such thing as an "easy" sale.

Even those sales that fall into place smoothly may only be the end product of a number of things: first, the accumulated knowledge and experience of all the training, education, and interviews which have gone before; second, the conveyance of all the confidence of an agent who feels comfortable in the particular selling situation; third, the preparation that has preceded the interview; and fourth, the experience that allows the exact filling of the exact solution to the exact need or problem, in other words, "an idea whose time has come." Finally, there are all the variables that go into this inexact science called selling.

Practically everything I've written so far has dealt with the approach. The real subject of this book is the "close," so

now let's close the "approach," and approach the "close."
Starting in Chapter Two and in all subsequent chapters, you
will find illustrations that I have developed, ideas which have
proved they work, and power phrases that sell. Most of the
material is original, although in the cerebral world in which
we work, ideas magically spring into our heads sometimes
without our knowing the stimuli.

If we take an opposite view, maybe nothing is original
since the whole subject of insurance springs from two
mathematical laws and nothing else: the law of large numbers
and the law of compound interest. Therefore, when one
assumes he has a new idea, he is only adopting some of the
tax climate in which we work—what the technical experts call
"Restatements and Reforms."

The illustrations used are designed to be closing ideas
that focus on the real issue. They are designed to be put on
one sheet only. The closing phrases and ideas are designed to
zoom in on one focal point only. In an interview, it may take
quite a while to develop the scenario to the point of using the
prepared material. The client's "yes" only comes in one
word, so our job is to find and expose the one simple thought
that earns that word. When we push the buttons on our tiny
hand-held calculator, the answer comes instantaneously, but
think of all the circuitry that goes into the fingertip-sized chip
in the machine. Think also of the fact that the only downsize
limitations on the calculators are screens large enough to read
the display off of and buttons big enough for our fingers to
use. Some of the buttons on the watch calculators are so
small that a stylus is needed to punch them. That is the purpose of my simplified sales aids: To find the smallest, but
most correct, hot button.

Consider the miles of wire and circuitry in one of the
large, sophisticated computers. Consider also the miracle of
the hand-held calculator. Both of them are only a manifesta-
tion of what goes on in a human brain. After all, the only
things that have gone into the programming of the machines

are the ideas of people. The advantage of computers lies in their capacity for storing many people's brain power and in their speed of recalling and displaying information on a screen. Therefore, all the eons of thought and miles of wire have undulated to print out what humans command, and to pinpoint exactly what is needed. This also is one of the intents of effective proposals: to jell thinking on the important issues. A good illustration, as a result, capsulizes many people's thinking right down to the instant.

In regards to the stories, humor, and philosophy herein, they're all mine. They come from being in the insurance business for 27 years and being associated with some pretty diverse but classy salespeople. I've spoken at company meetings, agency meetings, and life underwriters' meetings. I've been out among you and I report that you are a quality breed of folks. I was warned about the "hicks" in some of the small towns and of the pushy people in the Big Apple. I attest to you that there is no difference. I did not spot the shortcomings or the long looks. We may speak differently in various parts or the country, but it ends right there, with the accents, twangs, and drawls. The willingness of the life insurance cadre to share with their clients is only a part of the giving and sharing that takes place. You make things happen by sharing in the civic and charitable areas of your operations. But most of all you share with each other with a willingness that salespeople in other fields just cannot understand.

Most of what I chronicle in this book has been shared with me by you. I'm only the storyteller. A small part is my own, and I give that freely to be used as you see fit. Hopefully, you can make improvements so that someone else can profit by your added value. Incidentally, if you piggyback on some of my ideas and it works, send me a copy. I would be interested in all improvements so that I can use them in the second, third, and subsequent generations of brain power.

All of these ideas were not closers and I have my strike-outs just like any other salesperson. When I refer to one of these, I will be honest with you and reveal that this is the case or idea that did not work out. The biggest thrill in selling does not come in making the sale. It comes with the anticipation of making the sale. If there were no chance for missing, there would be no expectation and our profession would be a mechanical job and would have a corresponding hourly rate. That, we do not have and, for this reason, there must be as much of a possibility of missing a sale as there is of making one.

To stay healthy, one of the things that is required is a sense of humor. We must be able to laugh at ourselves continually. You know why? Because we are pretty darn funny. Some of our travails may seem earth-shattering at the time they occur, but what difference will it make 10 years from now? So I throw in some kidding. . . . Laugh along . . . even out loud. It vouldn't hoit!

*   *   *

2.

LEAD ME DOWN THE PATH

Everyone always promises that on the morrow, they are going to get organized. Everyone has a system for going about daily business and personal routines. Even no system is a system. It's not a good system, but it is a system. It systematically stays away from organization. There are those who thrive on being buried in the middle of their work, with piles and files all around them. That way, if you have a good swivel chair, you can whirl in every direction, almost drilling yourself into the floor, all the while reaching out for projects that need doing. Also, under this method, one needs lots of desktop, tabletop, and credenza space to accommodate the ever-increasing mounds of paper. Invariably, these persons also run out of furniture tops, so they start filing on chairs and ultimately, the floor. These people are perfectly comfortable in this mayhem, and can truly be organized in their disorganized fashion. They always admonish the staff, cleaning people, and others, "Don't touch anything; I know where everything is." And they usually do, although sometimes it takes Sherlock Holmes-type sleuthing to find something or helter-skelter admonitions and accusations to pin down something that, "I put right there, who took it?"

I can think of three people for whom I have the utmost respect and love who fall into this category: George Steinberger, J.D., CLU; my friend, Price Gaines, CLU, of the National Underwriter Co.; and my spouse, Sharon Meisel, C.B.W. (Certified Best Wife). George even has a sign on his desk that says, "A Cluttered Mind Is a Sign of Genius." Most times, however, the sign cannot be seen because of the other symbols of George's genius covering it.

Price Gaines is the life and health editor for the National Underwriter Co., and we must excuse his dust because if there ever was a place where a paper explosion should hit, it's most assuredly a journalist's office. On a recent visit, I was amazed at how Price was able to find exactly the books or references we wanted in *Tax Facts* and the National Underwriter publications.

My wife, Sharon, falls into this category too. Her bastion of collectibles is the "junk drawer." I think every house has one of these, so I won't explain it, although I may proclaim it and advertise it when we try to sell the house. Our junk drawer has been the hiding place for everything from grocery coupon offers to three-cent U.S. postage stamps (discovered in 1981, no less) to some official-looking pieces of plastic that no one seems to know what they do, but they're too good to throw out. I also suspect that someday, the F.B.I. will raid our house and find seven of the "Ten Most Wanted Criminals" in our junk drawer. But once again, and with the most genuine sincerity that I can muster by the written word, I say Sharon has done two things eminently well: she has raised four beautiful daughters and kept me on track for 28 years.

The watchword for these types of people should be a plaque or card saying, "Next week, I'm going to get organized." Actually, by next week they wouldn't be able to find the plaque or card.

The opposite of these people is the "neatnik," into which category I fall, along with about 50 percent of the world's population. The symbiosis between Type A and Type

B people is astounding. They "can't stand" each other, but they "can't do without" each other either. So for me, "A" stands for "agenda" and I try to organize my selling on a structured basis by use of agendas.

The use of an organized format does a number of useful things: primarily, it saves time, eliminates mistakes, and offers a permanent record. The time-savings come as a bonus to both the client and the agent. How many times have we gone on an appointment or delivery and forgotten to get a form signed or get some information that we needed? We arrive back at our office after the heat of battle, start to sort out the file, and notice we forgot the very amendment form we went out to get. But we did get the check. So now we have to think seriously about whether or not the item is important enough for us to go ourselves . . . can we send someone else . . . can it be done quickly enough by mail . . . can it wait for another meeting? It's times like these that bring out the wiliness, craftiness, nastiness, or self-anger that are merely reactions to a situation that could have been avoided initially with only a little bit of prethought. The decision is made a little simpler and faster if the gentle compulsion of "no payment of commissions until all requirements are met" gets thrown into the transaction. Consider also what the client will think when you call back, talking fast and trying not to stutter about how someone else failed to prepare you fully to complete the dealings. Most times, it sounds like a con job. Truth rings loudest, but insincerity also sends a message.

Another phase of the time-saving and mistake-elimination aspects is the beautiful businesslike quality of organization. The best public speakers are those who tell their audiences what they're going to say, say it, and then review what they have said. To convey that message lucidly to their listeners, accomplished speakers organize and outline their speeches carefully beforehand. Does this really differ from the steps we take when we are getting ready for an interview, be it for a crowd of one thousand listeners or an audience of one prospect? Even if it is only one person, as it is most of the time, we are still making a speech, trying to influence thought in a preconceived fashion. Therefore, it makes the clearest sense to me to make this "winning formula" outline in advance so that I can do the job efficiently and right. I often spend up to two hours getting an agenda in the exact order I feel is right for an interview, even after I have spent many earlier hours gathering all the research material.

I make my agendas so that the flow of ideas is in the order I think is right. The items on the agenda may consist of only a few words each and may have additional material supporting each point, but the initial report is almost always contained in one page. On that page, I explain the primary purpose of the meeting, the primary points to consider, and the primary solutions. Since I am always present at the interview, this acts as my outline while I make my oration. The object is simplicity; it is important to write down only what is really important. One page should do it. I feel if the agenda ever takes more than one page, the only words to appear on page 2 should be, "Do not write on this page."

In the agenda, I include all the things that have to be done, either by me or someone else, including the client, his advisers, or insurance companies. Everything that has to be done or that I want considered is outlined. I insert summaries of proposals, policies, correspondence, future action items, and collection of new checks or old premiums. Medical examinations and applications are mentioned routinely, just as if they were the next order of business—and frankly, they are. That is one of the purposes of the agenda, to make the whole meeting seem exactly like a boardroom situation, with each item having a prepared place of importance of its own. After all, the changing of a beneficiary on an old policy is just as important to the policyholder as the discussion of new insurance as outlined on the agenda. The listener can see that the preplanned meeting will do the quickest and most efficient job. He or she can see that I place equal emphasis on all aspects of the program.

Therefore, the main purpose of the agenda is to give me a track to run on and to get everything done that requires doing. If I have brainstormed my interview well enough, the actual meeting should go as I want it to go. I will accomplish all the service items, new items and, very importantly, future items. The agenda will list all the things that have to be done, but at the end of the prewritten agenda, there will always be one or two blank numbers where I can insert those items that arise as a result of this session. If the client mentions something to which I wish to respond, I have two choices: I can do so immediately or I can defer it, whichever makes the most sense. If I want to defer, I tell the client that it is a good point or question and put it under one of the blank points so that I don't forget it. If I don't know the answer, I ask the client to write it down in his or her agenda and I do the same in mine so that I remember to research it later. At this juncture, the client feels very important because he or she is contributing to the meeting, but even more important to me is the fact that the interview is becoming a dialogue and not a one-sided affair. The client shows more interest because he or she now feels an obligation to complete the entire agenda so that we cover their points as well.

Another plus for the agenda is permanence. This applies to the client as well as me. For our purposes, you know how vital it is to keep accurate records. To the client, however, I convey the idea that it is just as necessary, especially if it is a business client. I tell the client to punch holes in this paper and make it a permanent part of the corporate minute book. It is not an ironclad law that all items in this company book be prepared by a lawyer. Other professionals are happy to look at the agenda of an insurance meeting prepared by an agent, along with the personal, handwritten notes of the client. If the client or I have not had contact with the corporation's other advisers, they are more easily filled in by a written record of the meeting, even if it is not recorded in beautiful prose. I'm surprised to see that sometimes my agendas are the first writings ever to appear in some of these supposed ongoing records. I also find that a certain sense of pride of ownership, individuality, and stewardship comes over the business principal when he or she unlocks the mystery of the "corporate minute book" and makes an entry.

To me, the agenda is as much a part of being an agent as being neatly dressed and carrying a decent briefcase are. My method of presentation is superior to dragging some stray thoughts out of the air and letting the whole meeting fall into some haphazard malaise. Other professionals who have not done any preparation for the meeting lose ground to me because I have gained control. If my agenda is a well-thought-out one, other agents can't find many areas to sharp-shoot and they rise to a higher plane than they might otherwise by being constructive and positive and adding to the discussion, rather than trying to capture it.

The agenda is one way of controlling the interview, but another method which adds immeasurably is an overhead projector. It is almost like, "Who's wearing the tie?" What I am referring to in this area is authority symbolism. I have a client who owns a chain of medium- to low-priced furniture stores. The salesmen in these stores are not really the highest class guys, and there is no dress code except for who wears the tie on which days. The guy with the tie plays floor manager that day. If customers come in with complaints or service needs, they are all sent to him. The other salespeople just say, "See the man with the tie." It's goofy, but it works. Of course, the tie revolves daily, but this little authority symbol gives the wearer more respect in the eyes of the buyer since he is the only one sporting it. Think about it for a second. Even a large chain store run by a squad of teenagers working for minimum wage takes on some decorum if they get dressed up in red coats. (This is especially true if they have one of those pocket shields filled with pencils, pens, tire gauges, and other assorted paraphernalia that no one else has.)

The kid working in a discount department store and being asked to wear a tie or a linen coat enjoys doing it. He is set somewhat apart from the other people in the store's employ. The mark of difference is important and gives a feeling of responsibility to the wearer. He knows that all eyes are upon him. He enjoys that and tries to rise to a higher plane in giving service or answering questions. The same thing holds true for both male and female agents who wear business suits. The business suit means just that—business. It is looked upon as a symbol of preparedness and an announcement of what the purpose of the instant encounter is. I keep my jacket on almost all the time. I feel more businesslike and I get treated that way. In my office I wear my jacket whether or not there are clients in for meetings. I have often had people comment on how nice I dress or how nice my suit looks—even on days when I would not have agreed with them. I think every one of us has an outfit that should be thrown out, but we like it and so continue to wear it. On days when I have worn one of these uniforms, I have still received compliments. What was really going on was a recognition of something different and maybe not real admiration for my attire. I think I get a higher measure of respect from my associates and my staff when my garb proclaims to them that I am here for a purpose, and I expect the same from them.

This goes for the guy who keeps his jacket on in business meetings. I know that I may get a lot of arguments here from people who say that the ones who take off their jackets and roll up their shirtsleeves look like they are ready for work. It may be more comfortable and it may look more involved to rip off the outer cover, but there is no doubt of the effectiveness of being the one in control and saying so just by your outside advertising. If you don't go along with this notion, field-test it sometime. Leave your coat on while everyone else takes theirs off. Try and notice the difference in voice level, courtesy, and compliance between those who undress and those who stay collected. It's good to be one of the guys or gals when the clients relax in their work environment, but you'll carry more credence when everyone else assumes one posture and you assume another. I also understand fully that nothing in life is one hundred percent and there are those among you who go to work in jeans and purple velvet jumpsuits. So I say to you, that for you, you're probably right and keep up what works well for you. However, for the overwhelming majority of "conformists," leave your vestments on.

My point above is that very few agents spend a lot of time preparing for a meeting. When the client is faced with someone who has prepared an outline and controls the setting, it only makes sense to listen and act in a serious and thoughtful fashion. To further orchestrate my meetings, I use the overhead projector anytime I have more than two people in on a meeting. This is true whether the meeting is at our office or outside. My machine is portable and it paid for itself the first time I used it—and over and over again ever since.

I'm going to illustrate some agendas in the next chapter, but now I want to summarize the use of these with a final instruction. The purpose of the agenda is to win whatever we are after in that interview. If we need back-up paper, it should be available. But full disclosure is not a requisite of the synopsis. In most cases the customer only wants to know the final score, not the details of the game. When one asks the time, he or she doesn't care how the watch was made. Brevity is the key word here.

One of the best examples of synopsis writing with which we're all familiar is the TV guidebook that comes with the Sunday newspaper. Almost anyone can get the full theme of a show just by a few words. This is precisely my purpose in steering the prospect's brain channel to the proper picture, just as the TV guidebook does in getting our eyes on the right channel. Consider how difficult some people find explaining a movie that the other party has not seen. They start in the middle, repeat themselves, generally take too long, probably oversell and, in the end, make seeing the movie a low-priority item.

Consider also how the TV copywriters, because of space restrictions, can tell everything you have to know about a long movie and do it in only one sentence. For example: " 'Homecoming,' 1948, Clark Gable, Lana Turner. A society doctor learns new values on the battlefield when her sidekick nurse dies. (2 hr., 30 min.)" That is really a beautiful piece of condensation and is exactly what I try to impart in the items of my agendas. I want to lead to a conclusion, but I don't want to discourage interest. Let's now look at a few actual agendas and the explanations of the concepts being discussed or the unique features of one agenda as compared to another.

*   *   *

3.

WHO'S IN CHARGE HERE?

A football team needs a quarterback, a band needs a leader, a company needs a president, and each meeting where there is something to accomplish must have someone to give the session guidance. We have talked about taking charge and acting and directing the part. Most meetings start late and end late. Few are efficient and complete all the work on the agenda. It would be almost impossible to meet all the criteria of time and efficiency, without planning ahead. In producing a TV or radio show, everything gets done on time or it just doesn't get aired. This is one reason why there are hardly any live shows, excluding sports and special coverages, and why almost everything is now on video or audio tape. What has to get done, gets done within the allotted time.

A lot of material gets left on the cutting-room floor and there is a lot of rehearsal until the producers feel that the product is right. In conducting our business interviews, why not try to come as close as we can to presenting our views and getting action taken. The proposals and ledger statements that spew out of our computers give us the information we need, along with all the math and logic that support the data. In addition, we get ready for some of our encounters by gathering what we call back-up material to substantiate or create a viewpoint. I do considerable research in preparing a case but my goal in selling is to get the job done as efficiently and rapidly as possible. I once heard a 100-meter dash runner, after winning a race, explain to the commentator that he had not run a good race. The perplexed interviewer asked why the runner felt that way. He was told that in running the perfect race, "There should be nothing left when it's over." In this instance, the sprinter was tired but he wasn't exhausted. That's easy for him to say and maybe even harder to do, but running is closer to exactitude than selling is. The runners know the precise distance and the condition of the course. The only real opponents are themselves on the particular day and the conditioning that they have put into themselves before the race starts. The other runners are on the track but they are only a part of the factors for winning. Most of the inertia and resistance comes from within the runners themselves.

In selling, appointments are akin to running a known distance; we know where we want to end but the exact course is not known. Our resistance comes not only from ourselves, but also from the public. The agendas I prepare are for the purpose of getting "from here to there" in the shortest possible time and on the best possible route. I may spend 10 hours preparing for a 10-minute meeting, as opposed to spending 10 minutes for what may turn out to be a series of interviews totalling 10 hours.

In this chapter, I will show you some actual agendas prepared for interviews. The names, places, and other private information have been blocked out to protect the confidentiality of the client, but the rest of the copy is just as it was presented. I will explain my desires, aims, and methods.

The agenda serves the same purpose as an agenda for any corporate boardroom situation. The main topics and subissues are enumerated, and there are varying amounts of explanations that must be done when I present the case. We still need people to sell insurance. The machine at the airport that sells airline travel accident insurance can't replace us yet.

I'll make one more small observation, then get into showing some of the agendas that have worked for me and some that haven't. Lest any reader get the idea that these are foolproof, let me repeat what you have heard before. You can't sell them all. The law of averages still works. I try to get the odds on my side by doing the interview analysis, brainstorming, visualization, and review prior to the time I have to do it for real. As I stated above, a prepared or "canned" interview is not necessarily a bad thing, if that is what is required. My agendas could be called my "canned" talk with variables anticipated and welcomed. The primary observation is that these scripts work for me and that is the only recommendation I make. If you can use them as a basis for improvement please do. If you improve on them, please share —drop me a line. If you try them and they aren't working quite right and you would like some help, call me. I'll try to assist you. You can get my address from the MDRT roster.

I now refer to the agenda I have labeled illustration 1. This was a rather simple agenda but one which contained a lot of work to be done. Item 1 refers to a review of insurance that was in force for two years. It looks like an innocuous little entry that could be a part of any interview. The purpose was to review the buy-sell agreement and the funding, but the real goal was to plant two seeds. One was to show how little the program was really costing, and the other was to get the future insurance on William with me as opposed to his former company. When the case was first sold, William insisted on buying his policy from a company in his own hometown, about a thousand miles from Michigan which is the head office of the corporation. There was no dissuading him from having his policy set up with this nonpar company.

Illustration 1.

B———S, INC.

AGENDA — MARCH 7, 1983

1. Review of Connecticut Mutual In-Force Insurance

2. Review of Projected Stock Redemption & Full-Funding
   Insurance

   a) Requirements

   b) New Specs

3. Discussion of Key-Man Plans

4. Discussion of Deferred Compensation Plans

5.

6.

Illustration 2 is not an agenda but a display of the details of the policies already in force. Since it was the graphic discussed in point 1 of the agenda in illustration 1, I will explain its purpose and use now. One way or another, we have all used a sheet of this type to demonstrate a series of policies. I put a couple of things in this display that are different from just having a review of policies. The "out-of-place" columns are numbers 2, 10, and 11. These refer to the shares of stock issued by the corporation, the same ones which are to be repurchased according to the stock-redemption agreement. Column 2 ("Issued Shares Owned") is simple; it merely lists the number of shares owned by the individual shareholders.

In column 10 ("1983 Cost Per Share"), I divided the "1983 Cost" from column 9 by the total number of shares, 66,668. This gave the result labeled as "1983 Cost Per Share." Column 11 ("1984 Cost or Gain Per Share") was calculated using figures I left off this illustration in the interest of clarity. If I had displayed them, however, they would have been determined by figuring the 1984 cost or gain and dividing by 66,668. The obvious factors were that the total insurance package was costing 10.34¢/share, while the policy on William was costing 10¢/share on its own. In the interview I made these observations, but I did not make a large issue of them.

For item 2 of the agenda in illustration 1, I had another display of the value of the corporation at the moment and what the premium would be to fund the entire new package. I showed William the package of another company that had a lower premium, a higher cash value, and dividends, in addition. "Cost per share" is language that businesspeople readily understand. These are terms that they use every time they do an analysis of the financial papers of the business. Therefore, my interjecting this relationship into the insurance spreadsheet was accepted as a natural thing by them. It also made our insurance terms easier to understand since they now related to the client's usual and customary terms. Item 2 also

Illustration 2.
B——S, INC.
CONNECTICUT MUTUAL INSURANCE COMPANY

Insured	Issued Shares Owned	Policy #	Face Amount	1983 Cash Value	1984 Cash Value	One Year Increase	1983 Premium	1983 Cost	1983 Cost Per Share	1984 Cost Or Gain Per Share
Larry	15,334	3791580 (CML)	$125,952	$ 3,898	$ 5,888	$1,990	$ 2,098	$ 108	.001¢	.0002¢ Gain
Joe	10,667	3791582 (CML)	125,952	4,208	6,351	2,143	2,159	16	.0002¢	.0011¢ Gain
Terry	10,000	3791583 (CML)	82,143	1,734	2,638	904	924	20	.0002¢	.0002¢ Gain
Don	15,334	3791584 (CML)	87,619	3,282	4,945	1,663	1,862	199	.002¢	.0018¢ Cost
William	15,333	00-1067481	$126,000	—0—	—0—	—0—	6,673	6,673	.10¢	.1076¢ Cost
TOTALS:	66,668		$447,666	$13,122	$19,822	$6,700	$13,716	$7.016	.1034¢	.1061¢ Cost March 1983

refers to "cost per share," although I will not go into too much detail regarding what was in this item. The key thing was the reference to something that they understand and that is from their vernacular and not just from ours. The effect of the agenda was that the interview went very smoothly since there was complete clarity about the purpose of the insurance. Because everything was on a "dialogue" level, as opposed to a "lecture" level, a sale resulted from all the recommendations that I made in item 2.

Items 3 and 4 indicate what was discussed and I'll not go into these points under this discussion of agendas. Item 4 was not acted upon, but item 3 was. The result of this interview was a substantial increase in stock-redemption insurance and a new placement of key-man insurance. The whole meeting was a rather long one since there was a lot of material to be discussed, but it would have taken a lot longer and may not have had the same conclusion if I had not had the agenda prepared in advance of the meeting.

Illustration 3, Basic Pension and Follow-up Interview, shows an example of one agenda being used on two different interviews. The typewritten copy was used on August 22, 1977. The interview was being done by Bill Clancey, CLU, and myself. Bill had not yet met the client and his CPA.

Item 1 introduced our firm to the client. Items 2, 3, and 4 were very basic discussions concerning the types of plans, the taxability, and the investment media. Item 5 introduced Tom Connor, who was the brokerage manager of Bankers Life of Iowa, which is the company we were using for the retirement plan deposit of $20,000. Item 6 was a very interesting, condensed way of showing that because there were three highly paid employees, the profit-sharing benefit to the sole shareholder was not a big one in relation to total deposit. So under item 6(B) we suggested $250,000 of whole life insurance on a deferred compensation basis. Obviously this is not a deductible item, so we explained to our client that the total cor-

Illustration 3. Basic Pension and Follow-Up Interview

RED - Sept. 7, 1977

AGENDA — AUGUST 22, 1977
SPE———Y CARTAGE, Inc.

1. Introduction of Clancey and Meisel firm

2. General discussion of retirement plans—IBM

   a. Contributions deductible
   b. Accumulations tax-free
   c. Income payouts tax-favored

3. Two kinds of plans

   a. Defined Benefit
   b. Defined Contribution

4. Types of investments

5. Banker's Life of Iowa Plan

   a. Tom Connor

6. Combination Plan—Bill Clancey

   A. $20,000 Profit-Sharing—all employees
   B. $ 5,000 Selective Salary Continuance—Bill only

7. SWAG (B.D.)

8. Integrated-Profit-Sharing Plan

9. Disability-Paul Revere

10. Steps To Be Taken
    a. Corporate Resolution
    b. Forms
    c. Bank Deposit In Name Of Trust
    d. Medical Examination

porate contribution was really $30,000, including the profit-sharing plan, with $20,000 as a deduction. The client was very happy with this form of combination plan, because the greatest contribution and benefit share was for him. He could also say to his employees that they were getting as much from the profit-sharing plan as he was. The CPA said he would need a few days to prepare the final census list, so we set up the next meeting for September 7, 1977.

For the follow-up meeting, we used the photocopies of the earlier agenda. In the second meeting, we used the first six points to review our first session. The handwritten copy starting with item 7, and the legend at the top, **"Red"—September 7, 1977,"** was the completion of the earlier interview. Item 7 referred to a remark that the client (B.D.) made at the first meeting. When we were asking for information in the fact-finding stage, he said, "That would be SWAG." I had never heard the statement before, so he defined it for me as a "Scientific Wild-Assed Guess." He was proud of having introduced something new to us, so I put it into the second interview to kick off items 7 and 8, which now pinpointed the rough figures they had given us earlier into a final retirement-plan proposal.

Item 9 was a disability presentation and item 10 completed the transaction.

Illustration 4, Combined Agenda, depicts an extremely busy interview. It accomplished a tremendous volume of work that had to be done. The interview was with two men who owned all of the shares of C——C, Inc., and a partnership, ——ORD Development, both on a 50-50 basis. I had already sold them stock-redemption insurance for the corporation and partnership insurance. At this meeting I wanted to plant the seed for a retirement plan and tie in the estate planning. I had told them at the very first meeting we had that my areas of work were business planning, retirement planning, and estate planning. I also pointed out that taking care of any

Illustration 4. Combined Agenda

C————C, INC.

AGENDA — NOVEMBER 1, 1979

1. Review Stock Redemption Funding:

   a. Comparison Sheets Term and Permanent
   b. Value $200,000—Insurance Complete
   c. Get Agreement Redrawn Stating Price and Listing Insurance Policies
   d. Aviation Rider for P——.
   e. Forms and Check—$550.50
   f. Deliver Four Policies
   g. Return M————H Policy

2.

3.

——ORD DEVELOPMENT

1. Review July 14, 1979 Agenda

2. Review Partnership Funding

3. Forms and Checks—$1,807.00

4. Deliver Two Policies

5.

RETIREMENT PLAN

1. Defined Benefit, Profit-Sharing, or Both

2. Amount of Deduction Desired

3.

PERSONAL ESTATE PLANNING

1. Almost Completed When Other Programs Done

---

two of the three almost completed the third one automatically. This was true as long as all the planning and insurance placement was done in a proper legal and tax frame.

Item 1 concerned the corporation only. Under 1(a), my purpose was to put the permanent policies that I had ordered out first, rather than the term policies, which had also been requested. At the first meeting, the type of coverage became a discussion point and almost got to the stage where nothing would be done, so I told them that the type of coverage we were considering did not make too much difference and that we should concern ourselves with the protection aspect first. The sheet that I used for illustrative purposes showed the cost aspects of the term policies and the savings aspects of the permanent. I made the strong argument that it was usual to prepare for a stock redemption for both a death and a living situation. I explained that this was usually done with the same dollars through a permanent policy that would, of course, pay at death, but at the same time would stockpile dollars that could be used during life to redeem stock either because of a complete termination of the business, or a buyout when one or the other of them decided to retire or sell. Good logic prevailed and I placed the permanent policies. The illustration I used was the same type of computer comparison of term versus permanent which all of the readers can get from their own computer sources. It is not important to this basic discussion of the use rather than all of the attachments to an agenda and I have not reproduced it here.

Item 1(c) indicated that the agreement in force, which did not have any language regarding death funding, should be updated both for language and the listing of the insurance policies under a schedule in the agreement. I realize that this point in the agenda does not say all of that. Remember my explanation of the purposes of agendas, one of which is to give me a track to run on while at the same time getting the client's mind in gear in an orderly fashion.

Another purpose of the agenda is to enumerate all the things that have to be done at this meeting, therefore, the necessity for items 1(d), (e), and (f). These reminded me to pick up the aviation rider form for one of the shareholders who was paying a surcharge for his flying activities. I also needed additional money in the amount of $550.50 to complete the semiannual premium. Item 1(f) reminded me to leave only the correct policies. Notice how all the items that I want to show are spelled out without any intent to hold back information. I want them to get used to the idea that cash and paper are required, and I want it approached in a routine, businesslike fashion both by me and by the clients.

Item 1(g) was just a matter of reminding me to return the policy which was already in force and which I had reviewed.

Items 2 and 3 were left blank in case anything came to light that had to be taken care of at a later time or a later meeting. There were no future items in this first part having to do with the corporation, so we moved on to the partnership.

The partnership, here referred to as ——ORD DEVEL-OPMENT, required quite a bit of conversation. Since this was going to be a long agenda in any event, I did not want to risk losing our train of thought because of tedium, so I referred to the agenda that we first used on July 14, 1979, when the sale was first made. This way, I could force a break in the action by getting on to a second sheet but still appear to be presenting only one sheet that was not too long. The individual items were much the same as for the corporation and I had the amendment forms signed, picked up the balance of the premium due, and delivered the policies. A couple of things deserve special notes: first, I did not make too much of an issue over amendment forms. I just referred to them as "forms." It so happened that one of them was for health and required part of the $1,807.00 in item 3. The other form was, once again, the flying rider for the other partner. We covered the fact that we expected a health rating on the first interview and I handled it routinely on this agenda by the word "forms." This is not to say that there was no discussion, but it was not a surprise and I did not make a large issue over it.

The third part of this agenda had to do with a retirement plan and I approached it just as you see in the illustration. Rather than talking about the choice of whether or not to have one, I discussed the two varieties and the amount of deduction desired. They decided on item 2 first, and when we knew the amount, we talked about all the factors affecting this company, such as: number of employees, stability, history of profits, and relative wages of the shareholder/employees as compared to the other employees. Our conclusion was to install a profit-sharing plan. I left a census list for the secretary to complete, and we moved on to the last item on the agenda.

"Personal Estate Planning" was almost as easy as it looks listed here. It only deserved one line since, as I said before, when two of the three legs are finalized the third is almost done too. I suggested that we should have individual meetings for the personal estate planning, but they told me their values were almost the same and they wished to talk generally while we were all together. We discussed the fact that the corporation was now liquid, as was the partnership. All that was really needed was the exercise of paperwork with the attorney for the business document fine-tuning and the drafting of new wills and trusts. Over our three meetings together we had a general consensus on the approximate taxes due for estate clearance and transfer, and I told them this was not a great amount and that we could take care of it on a deductible basis through insurance owned by the profit-sharing plan. They agreed and I told them I would have the proposed plan drawn up with a couple of different insurance designs. They agreed, once again, and we terminated what could have been a confusing meeting by leaving the paperwork and the retirement plan for the next interview.

This agenda took about one hour to design. It was not hard in itself because I had one to follow from the first interview. That one also took about one hour to design. Therefore, I had about two hours of agenda preparation time involved in two meetings that took a total of about three and a half hours to conduct. Of course, there was other work, such as reading the existing documents and preparing rate comparisons, but all of this was better done by me in the depths of my office rather than in front of the clients. We did a considerable amount of work in a relatively short period of time. After all, we covered two buyouts, a retirement plan, and estate planning. I have no doubt that I would have done a far poorer and slower, and even less efficient job had I not done all the thinking and brainstorming in my own backroom and then plotted it out in agenda form.

Illustration 5, Pictorial Agenda, was done for a corporation meeting that was held at the attorney's office. I knew only one of the shareholders, Gerry, so I was really in the position of having to sell myself to the corporation and attempting to close a sale on the very first interview. I did have a lot of information from Gerry, which allowed me to put together the outline that is pictured in illustration 5. You will notice that I put the names of the wives of the shareholders in parentheses next to the names of the owners. This is not the usual practice for me, but it was vital for the package I thought would fit for this company and the idea presented to them under item 4.

I had never met Dan, Ron, or the attorney, so my first job was to introduce myself. I did get introduced to Dan and Ron in the lawyer's waiting room, so we were already speaking by the time we got into the conference room and the meeting started. As usual when three shareholders get together with one another and their attorney, the buildup of facts that have not been discussed for a long while come forward and a conversation about business conditions and strategy commenced. I did not feel it was a bad thing to let this go on for a short while, because I wanted to know a little more about the personalities of the attorney and the two newly met stockholders. Also, I wanted to see if the attorney

Illustration 5. Pictorial Agenda

AGENDA—JULY 13, 1982

Corporation: C———
Shareholders: Gerry (Susan) — 55%
Dan (Pat) — 40%
Ron (Linda) — 5%

1. Introduction of Burt Meisel, CLU

2. Current "Retail" Plan — Unfunded

3. Considered "Wholesale" Plan — Funded

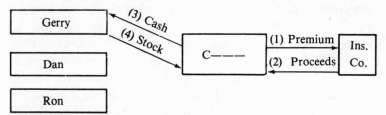

4. Bank Financing

   A) "Substitute Creditor"

5. Deferred Compensation

   A) "Exchange of Promises"

6. Premium Exhibit

7.

8.

would be the one to call the meeting to order and start it in an organized, knowledgeable fashion. I did learn a lot about the individuals during this under-talk time, and I determined that the attorney was informed on the subjects at hand, would not be an egocentric person, but would welcome a full sharing of ideas.

Gerry was the one to say that the meeting "might as well get down to business." At that point, I felt I wanted to lead this whole session, and I asked, "Would you like me to kick it off? I've prepared an agenda." On item 1, I spent about three minutes introducing myself and my firm by giving them my experience and credentials. I explained our alphabet soup: MDRT, CLU, Michigan Licensed Insurance Counselor, and so on.

Incidentally, I point out to all readers, it is extremely valuable to prepare a biography on yourself. I realize that the young, inexperienced person does not yet have all the credentials he or she will have in the future, but each of you does have some. People like to be assured that their choice in advisers is sound. Attorneys and doctors display every degree they own on their office walls. Some have more degrees than a thermometer and they spill over to the examining rooms. Some of the most boring reading I have ever done has been in one of these rooms when I forgot to take along a magazine from the waiting room and I was foolish enough to think that the doctor would be right along. About this time, one starts to examine the scrolls and engravings and pictures of ancient Greek gardens with the earliest-day jetsetters lolling around. But the sheepskins do their job; I'm always impressed with some of the side courses and refresher courses that my professional has taken. The feeling is that this person has tried and succeeded.

This philosophy has the same effect on our clients when we let them know we are achievers and winners. For those who have not gotten the educational designations or not yet qualified for the MDRT, put on your card what you have done. When your company sends you a plaque or certificate that denotes some selling club or high contest finish, use it to your advantage by putting it on your business card or other public relations material. If you have attended college, been a winner in some other industry, or done something unusual for the community, either civic or charitable, let people know. When you get further honors, replace those which do not mean as much. Psychologically, it is helpful for you to build your esteem a little at a time with the victories you have had. It takes away a little from the barrenness of lack of experience in the business. It also makes you a little more confident when you have just handed someone a sheet, card, or biography of your credentials. It reminds you that you are someone who has done something. It puts you in the frame of mind that you are a worthwhile person and that there is substance and reason for doing business with you. If you don't have heavy or even medium credentials, your company has, so use its standing to boost your own.

Getting back to the agenda, item 2 was illustrated to show the present position of the corporation, which was both unwritten and uninsured. My purpose with many of the terms that I use in these agendas is to get the mind greased and ready to receive input. I do not attempt to tell the whole story. We've got plenty of services and books which do that for us; but none of them will ever replace a salesperson doing the job. The terms are designed to plant one main theme and at the same time arouse interest in seeing more. The word "unfunded" explains itself but "retail" certainly doesn't, except for the fact that given a choice anyone would rather pay wholesale. This is the way I would reason and this is the way I want to steer the circuitry in my listener's brain.

An illustration called "Retail-Wholesale," which is an exposition of the methods of transferring a business interest at death, will be printed below. For now, in illustration 5, I simply drew boxes representing the principals and the corporation. I explained that the fact that there is no connection between the boxes precisely demonstrates the result after death. The stock will be in the same box but someone else's name will be on the title and it will not be the other shareholders.

Item 3 shows the words "wholesale" and "funded." Even standing naked on a piece of paper, those words are nicer and warmer than "retail" and "unfunded." I then recite that the picture is the same as above; however, a new square is introduced labeled, "Ins. Co." The sequence of events at death would be as follows:

1. "C—" sends premiums to the "Ins. Co."
2. "Ins. Co." sends proceeds to "C—."
3. "C—" sends cash to "Gerry's" box.
4. "Gerry's" box, his estate, sends his stock to "C—."

This eliminates Gerry's interest in the business and the other two boxes own the business in the same proportion they held before. I realize this is a "Sesame Street" type of approach to a big sale of a business, but it comes out clear and it is universally understood. Notice that, so far, we have not even discussed the value of the business or the premium figures required. At this point all I want to lecture about is concepts.

Item 4 was a shopping list item I threw in because I knew they had bank debt. The concept of the "Substitute Creditor" is for the spouse to own insurance on the life of his or her shareholder/spouse, who then receives tax-free payments from the corporation. This changes nothing for the corporation, which had to pay something anyway. It now makes loan repayments to a different creditor. They are still deductible to the company, but are nontaxable to the recipient, since it is not income but repayment of a debt. I will not reproduce this illustration, since it is not original with me. You can get copies of it from the MDRT, which is where I first saw it years ago. Since I now wanted to talk about spouses owning policies, I did not want to use impersonal terms like "your wife," so I learned the names in advance and that is why I had them at the top of the agenda next to the husband's name. It also helped me in not making mistakes in matching the wrong parties.

Item 5 was another shopping list point. Since I did not know where this interview would lead or if I could make a sale at this initial meeting, I was planting seeds of corporate planning benefits that could be sold later. The reference to "Exchange of Promises" is one of my illustrations and I will demonstrate it later.

As I mentioned, I did not know an awful lot about this company. One of the missing pieces was the value. I got to the numbers of the meeting by having a $100,000 illustration on a term-permanent spreadsheet, which I call "Increasing-Decreasing Premium." This is one of my basic and original illustrations and I will explain that one in a later chapter. By showing a sample amount of $100,000, it was easy to do mental math to fit the amounts needed. Here were the results of the conference: item 3, $350,000 of term insurance to cover buy-sell purposes. Item 4 was not a hit with them. They did not like the "Substitute Creditor" idea; instead, they wanted the corporation to have the option of paying off the debt or not, as dictated by bank negotiations at the time. Therefore, we set up $500,000 of term for the purpose of "key-man" benefits. Policies were owned by and paid to the corporation. They also agreed to large disability policies on the two shareholders who also were employees.

With the cost of today's term, this was not a gigantic sale in dollar amount, but it was in gaining a client with all the future potential for business and referrals (which have already come in larger amounts than the original sale). The agenda did its job extremely well. The attorney was happy he had all that paperwork to do. The clients were happy; they were protected. I was happy.

*　　　*　　　*

4.

MY WAY

Every meeting that transpires generally has only one or two thoughts that, taken by themselves, summarize everything that went on. After the president gives a 45-minute speech on television and the loyal opposition has its chance to respond and the television news teams analyze what both parties had to say, the newspaper comes out the next morning with four words that compact what all the high-priced talent expounded upon: "President Wants More Arms." If you saw the show and you then went on to read all the coverage, you would agree that the headline summed it all up.

College course-description books describe in a few words what a whole year of study is going to entail. In most cases the students can legitimately anticipate and understand what the whole year of school is going to be like.

Just a word or two can have a significant impact on the entire nation. Think about what happens when farmers band together and picket the White House or Congress, carrying

signs reading, "Parity." I know it has something to do with
equality or taking from one side and giving to another. I really don't know all the issues, but if I were interested, I could
catch on quickly because I have this broad-brush image in my
mind of taking from the dreaded "haves" and giving to the
worthy "have-nots." I don't know who is getting equal treat-
ment and who is going to pay, but I do know someone wants
something shifted.

In labor disputes the word is "equity." Once again, I
don't know what that means when taken out of context, but I
get the picture that someone is feeling shortchanged and
wants to grab something from the other side. Will it really be
equity if the picketers win? I don't know, but they present a
powerful argument simply by saying the word "equity."
They used it before the other side and it sounds like something they should have. Why would anyone not want the
workers to have equity? It all depends on the definition, but
the ones who use the influencing word first are the ones who
gain public sentiment. This is exactly the purpose of advertising during a strike.

In teaching, the words are "quality education." Now,
who could be against that? We all want that for our children
but what does that mean? Do we not have it now? And would
a large pay raise, which seems to be the real issue, get it? No
matter whose side the observer aligns with in the dispute, I
think the teachers have drawn first allegiance because they
have stated their issue in terms that are nonassailable.

At one time, I was a member of a school board. In those
early years after collective bargaining came to the classroom,
the board did its own negotiations. I was the chief negotiator,
thrust into that job without any experience. Most of the issues were folly and did not merit discussion. The real items of
concern were more pay and less work. We had to listen to all
of the items because that is what bargaining is all about.
I could hardly wait until we finished the "noneconomic"

items so that the last two pages could be taken from the secret compartment in the briefcase and brought up on the table. These were the two or three acceptable formulas for the pay increases.

My only concern was not to bankrupt the education of the students and at the same time not to exceed the mandate of the public. In those days we held to the letter of the law regarding no deficit financing. My hidden guideline was to avoid a strike. I did this jousting for three years with three unions and never had the threat of a work stoppage. My method of doing this was through the use of one word, and that word was not even supposed to be mine. The word was "strike" and that belongs to labor and not management. When the going got sticky in some little issue upon which I could have agreed easily and not lost any ground, I started my word campaign by stealing theirs. Early in the negotiations when an argument, no matter how slight, fomented, I would say, "Art, that sounds like an important thing; I wish we could say 'yes,' but we can't, so put it down as the first item on your 'strike' list." The response was usually, "We're not going to strike; we don't have any strike list." I would retort, "Yes, you do; and if this thing is as important to you as you say it is, you should fight for it." Answer: "I told you; we're not going to strike." I countered, "YES, you will." "We will not," someone else chimed in. "Drop the item," said the chairman, to which I said, "I can't. It must be important to some of the teachers, otherwise the committee would not have brought it up; put it on the strike list."

We never had a strike or a hint of one. They would not have dared because it was no longer their ploy; it was what the school board wanted and apparently was not afraid of. All I did was use the word first so that they got my message in the big picture. This is exactly the point of my preparing and steering an agenda. I want MY message, which in reality is theirs too, put across in a fair, open, and informative fashion.

I have already discussed the reasons for and the importance of the agenda. For a little background, let me explain how I physically prepare one. I know we all lament about how much of our education we forget. If we only retained one-fiftieth of what we learned in grade school, we would never miss a question on the TV game shows. If we can think back to our kindergarten days, we are on the same level as when I construct an agenda.

I start with letter-size paper, colored pencils, scissors, cellophane tape, ruler, and other highly sophisticated, computer-age paraphernalia. This is the easy part. The tough part obviously is the thinking, study, and simplifying that go into getting ready. Illustrations 6 and 7 were prepared for the delivery of pension policy increases and the solicitation of both new business for the corporation and personal business for the wife of the chief stockholder. Take a look at the two agendas right now, and get the gist of the items I had to include. There were a lot of diverse things to be done, ranging from a $60,000 term conversion for a small $500.00 premium to picking up the year's pension contribution in the amount of $71,764.03.

When I have a great number of things that have to go on one agenda, I first lay them all out on my desk. I then list each of them, in pencil, on my pad or piece of paper. The order makes absolutely no difference. All I want is a start. I list each of them with a main title, such as, "Fund Deposit" or "Terminations." I touch them up after I first get them listed. When I have them all strung up and down my sheet, I then give them a number according to where I feel I want them placed in the priority. For instance, "Cost and Benefits" might have shown up on my first list in fourth spot but after studying the ranking, I felt it was good psychology to show that first since it was something that had to be done, and it was a usual item that we had discussed in the past. They were familiar with it. So I mark a "1" next to "Cost and Benefits," and I rename it "Review of Cost and Benefits."

If I make a mistake or want to change something, I either strike it over in pencil or cut it out with the scissors and glue it on a new sheet that I am starting. When some of these things are finished, they are not unlike the pasted-up first renderings of a newspaper galley sheet. There isn't much more to the physical construction of my schedule. After the brainstorming about what I want to accomplish is done, I then hand it to my secretary for typing. She knows my hand-writing and crossovers better than I do, and the completed agenda comes back to me in the formats that you are seeing here. With that in mind, let's move into illustrations 6 and 7.

At the top of the agenda and personal agenda (illustrations 6 and 7), you will see it is for the U——D Company and that the interview was held on July 31, 1980. The subjects to be covered were both personal and corporate, so I prepared two different agendas to keep the different areas separated and to have a break in the action after we finished with the corporation. On occasion, I will put the agendas for corporate and personal and even partnership entities on the same sheet, but in this case I wanted them taken individually.

Item 1 on the company agenda was a big one since it had to do with a rather large deposit for the retirement plan. I did have another sheet that showed the employees, their dates of retirement, and all the other things generally found in pension displays. The dollar figures that appear in item 2 also appeared in the cost and benefit sheet, but I wanted them highlighted, delineated, and simplified in the most compact way possible.

There is one significant thing in item 2. To the right of the figures that appear in the regular agenda, you will see the notation regarding figures amended in August 1980. The reason for this is that in the census list we received from the corporation, there was a mistake in the salary of an employee, J.O. I had to go back in August but all I did was use the previous agenda and showed the changes to the prin-

Illustration 6. Annual Pension Review

U——D COMPANY
EMPLOYEES RETIREMENT TRUST
AGENDA — JULY 31, 1980

1. Review of Cost and Benefits

2. Contributions

		Aug. 1980 Amended— J.O. Salary ($57,200)
A. Life Insurance		
Canada Life	$12,871.07	$12,871.07
1979 Conn. Mut. 4,086.78		
1980 Conn. Mut. 2,541.78		
Total Conn. Mut.	6,628.56	7,002.36
Total Insurance Premium	19,499.63	19,873.43
B. Investment Fund Deposit	50,616.60	51,890.60
C. Total—1980 Contribution	$70,116.23	$71,764.03

3. Terminations—Surrender Forms and Policies:

   A. H.O.
   B. Y.G.
   C. A.V.

4. Investment Fund—Connecticut Mutual:

   A. Review Material

5. Dividend Statement From Canada Life:

   A. Amounts To Be Credited to Employees

6.

7.

cipals by just touching up the original agenda that they had already seen and with which they were familiar.

Item 3 involved some housekeeping on terminating employees. This note was to remind me to pick up forms and policies. It was worth special note since I was asking them for considerable money at these meetings. This spot is where they get some of that money back into the fund by way of forfeitures.

Item 4 was also a selling point, since I was trying to get the side investment fund placed with Connecticut Mutual in an annuity. Under 4(A) I went over the material on the specifications of the annuity fund. It was a rather complex and involved statement, but I summarized it as routine business in item 4.

Item 5 was, once again, some routine paperwork that I had to deliver to the trustees concerning investment results from the dividends. They had asked me, prior to the time of the appointment, to prepare this item.

Illustration 7 had to do with some personal insurance planning for two of the principals. It appears very simple and almost without substance, yet a great deal of new business was conducted. Please recall, we had just finished the corporate agenda and this one was for the purpose of putting the final touches on an overall program that had been ongoing for a number of years. The significant aspect of this display is its straightforward format for getting forms signed and planting new seeds.

For the first shareholder, B.R., we had previously discussed disability insurance, and what you see under point 1 is the reminder to sign the application. The object of the sale was not to discuss whether or not to have the disability coverage, but to take advantage of all that was available. Point 1(A) is probably the quickest and most concise explanation of disability provisions that one would ever see. I don't know

Illustration 7. Finishing Touches—Agenda

PERSONAL AGENDA — JULY 31, 1980

B.R.

1. Sign disability application for maximum limits, without additional examinations

   A. $4,075 monthly income—90-day wait; pay to age 65; premium amount—$2,136.56

2. Estate planning date with C.N. after warehouse move

3. S.A.—convert $60,000 term policy
   See proposal—

4.

R.E.

1. Complete beneficiary change forms

   A. Company

   B. Policy numbers

2. Disability?

---

how it could be any shorter. One of the things that went on in the dialogue is the fact that this man had just been approved for insurance in the retirement plan and all that was required now was the signature.

The second item had to do with completing the rest of the estate planning, which would result in the need for additional insurance for estate taxes. I knew these policyholders were planning a major location move for their business. I also knew that if I suggested they see the attorney immediately, they would wait until after the move. (The reference to C.N. in item 2 is to the lawyer.) My purpose, therefore, was threefold: first, to plant the seed for the meeting; second, to let them know it could not be done immediately and I was sensitive to their needs; and third, to get the attorney involved since I knew that his feelings were that the planning was direly needed. He would have been a great supporter of more protection, and I wanted him to be the springboard for the application.

The third item suggested a conversion of $60,000 of term insurance on B.R.'s wife, S.A. I handled it routinely as if our discussion had a foregone conclusion, since it had been mentioned at the last meeting we had and not acted upon. I put it in this agenda and displayed it in one of my two-column, "Increasing-Decreasing" premium illustrations, which I will demonstrate later in the book in one of the proposal illustration sections.

Point 4, which was the last point to pertain to this shareholder, was left blank for any items that might have been brought up by him. There were none, so it remained vacant. Every one of the first three items was acted upon in exactly the fashion I suggested.

The bottom half of the agenda sheet is devoted to the second shareholder, R.E.. This was the other shareholder and trustee under the pension plan. It is not usual that I would discuss personal business applicable to two different people at the same meeting. However, R.E. is the personal confidant of B.R. and has always advised him regarding business and personal matters. He is a marvelous, caring person and is always cooperative.

At past meetings, I had suggested that we break up into individual sessions for the personal stuff, but they did not mind revealing to each other what the planning was. They share all their ideas, use the same advisers, and constantly compare notes. The first time I did business with them this way, I was a little uncomfortable, but I quickly realized they were sincere when they said they wanted to sit in on each other's meetings.

Under point 1 for R.E., I required some beneficiary change forms from him because of some recent will and trust changes. He had lost some policies, so item 1 was primarily to remind me to get the full and correct information. Remember that selling is one aim for my agendas, but so is keeping me on target with what has to be done.

In point 2, I questioned whether or not he would set up disability insurance based on previous statements he had made. Make no mistake about it, I was not being timid here. For sure, I was selling in a positive mode. I knew he would do exactly as his associate had done up above, but I was playing to a different set of emotions with him, and I wanted him to think the option was all his and he was not reacting clonelike to his associate. In this situation I was playing the ball game on their home court and with their rules, but I was pitching the fast, straight ball to one man and offering a change-of-pace pitch to the other. As I told you earlier, I would let you know when I struck out. This was one of those times. One man said yes and in the same meeting, with two very like-thinking men, the other said no. He has his own reasons and has not changed to this day.

Illustration 8 is a demonstration of an agenda that puts together a number of divergent thoughts into a final closing

Illustration 8. Putting It All Together—Agenda

L.A./A.N. COMPANY
AGENDA — DECEMBER 17, 1981
ATTENDING: C., H., R., and BURT MEISEL, CLU

1. Review of April 16, 1981 Agenda

   A. Point 1(A)—Needs
   B. Point 1(B)—Change in Estate Tax Law

2. Review of December 1, 1980 Agenda

   A. Point 1—Changed Stock Redemption Terms
   B. Point 2—Flow Chart

3. Review of Planning Meetings—R. and IBM

   A. October, 1981 Company Comparisons
   B. Split Funding Flow Chart—Explanation
   C. Term—Permanent Comparison Sheet—R.
   D. Connecticut Mutual Non-Smoker Display
   E. Insurance Option Sheet—December, 1981
   F. Completion of Final Papers—Connecticut Mutual and Charter Security—*BOB ANNUITY*

4. Meetings With Attorney For Agreement Review

   A. Schedule A

5. Funding For —d. Leasing—R.

   A. Partnership—Corporation Laws

6.

7.

8. Referrals

IBM Notes: Second-death, new-estate tax law costs.
   Partnership can't close; call Drollinger and discuss.

December, 1981

interview. I had dealt with three men who were the share-holders of a corporation and the partners in a business that leased the land and equipment to the corporation. The date at the top of the agenda is December 17, 1981. I had had three or four meetings with these people over a period of about a year. Each of them had expressed different desires regarding the transfer of the businesses at death; they were not able to agree on how it should be done. At the same time, we were in the doldrums of very poor economic conditions in Detroit during the same period. Business was slow, and although death stops it altogether, they were afraid to make a commit-ment regarding the very sizable premiums we were discussing.

I designed this agenda to coincide with the earlier one I had done. My purpose was to make this interview as comfort-able and familiar as I could. Points 1(A) and 1(B) were iden-tical in placement to the ones on April 16th. I also anticipated that they may have taken my advice regarding filing these agendas in the corporate minute book and that my previous agenda may appear at this meeting. (It did.) Remember, if you will, my advice about each interview containing a key word. The key word in any insurance situation, whether it is spoken or not, is "needs." In this case, I put the word right in the agenda under point 1(A). Because we had had these previous meetings, one could assume that everyone knew ex-actly what we were considering, but I took no chances; I brought the needs right out again and verbalized the thought. When I called on the interview of December 17th, I had good reason to do so, since the Economic Recovery Tax Act of 1981 (ERTA) had come into effect in the fall of 1981. I did not recite confusing code numbers and long rhetoric under point 1(B), just the fact that the estate tax law had changed. In my dissertation, I talked a lot about it, but in the agenda, I just referred to it, without comment. I just wanted to open up the thinking ducts and whet the curiosity.

Point 2 went further back into history, relating to an agenda of December 1, 1980. In this item, I showed the changes that occurred to the stock redemption and the flow of cash to the estates because of the changes in the law. I did this by using the earlier agenda, and striking out in pen those items that no longer pertained. Incidentally, on this interview I was using the overhead projector, and a handwritten strike-over on a typewritten acetate really shows up clearly. Therefore, if some changes have been made, they are visibly and audibly up front.

Point 3 was a potpourri of items that had been discussed between "R" and me. There were a couple of meetings that were attended by only the two of us and not the other shareholders. Every point that was brought up was recorded and either answered on the spot or saved until this meeting when all the decision-makers would be present. "R" was not empowered to make a decision by himself, although he was the person who was designated to gather all the information. In item 3, I called all these interviews "planning meetings," denoting that I felt all of them were necessary and usual steps leading to this meeting, which was for the intended purpose of finalizing the natural step of protecting the corporation.

In item 3(B), I referred to a "Split Funding Flow Chart." This was a comparison I made of universal life versus whole life on a minimum deposit basis with the borrowed money put into single-premium deferred annuities. I showed this comparison assuming the same rate of interest for both the universal life and the annuities. The reason I did this was to protect myself from any competition that might have appeared offering the universal life. At that time I was not a fan of universal life, and as it turned out, neither were the owners. They had followed it in the *Wall Street Journal* and other newspapers and periodicals. They liked the minimun deposit/annuity idea, but I gave them the choice.

Item 3(C) refers to a discussion I had with "R" comparing term with permanent. For this closing meeting, I prepared my two-column comparison of the two products, picking the cash-value column out of the illustration in 3(B). I gave full credit to "R" for having brought up this valid point, and we discussed why equity-producing products are a better vehicle for a stock-redemption arrangement. "H" then expressed his views on why he felt it was important to be "conservative and safe and make sure there is some money there in case one of us wants to retire and get bought out in 20 years." I complimented him on his philosophy and expanded on the idea of "double-duty dollars."

The other items are fairly uneventful, except 3(F). In this one I just assumed consent. In other words, I felt there had been enough talk and that our goal here today was to put a plan into effect. I made the signing of the papers a routine part of this subsection. I asked who was to be this year's annuity applicant. They selected Bob. I said to mark it on all the copies of the agenda, as you can see I did on mine. I then went forward and asked for signatures; they did not stop me.

There was an old buy-sell agreement in force that was perfectly suitable for the new insurance, and in point 4 I informed them it would be an easy task to contact the attorney and have the agreement updated to include the new policies.

Item 5 had to do with the partnership. In it I spoke of the need to fund the partnership because of the same reasons we had just gone through for the corporation. I thought it would be foolish to mention anything else except that problems could occur. Therefore, there was no copy regarding anything. I relied on my saying that the problems could not be fully solved if the partnership were not liquefied. Primary among those problems was the fact that the estate could not be closed while the partnership interest was not settled. This meant ongoing expenses for administration and other problems attached to delay.

Points 6 and 7 are the usual blank spots for items that arise during the meeting. Point 8 is as blunt as I could make it. The interview itself resulted in a very large sale. But the job would only have been half-done if I had not asked for referrals. They were there just for the asking. The client feels good having just made a worthwhile decision regarding his financial and business planning. While he is still on a high regarding all the good things that have just transpired, why not let him share some of that exuberance by recommending some other firms that should have the same kind of service.

In the "Telling Like It Is" agenda (illustration 9), my purpose was to lecture a couple of people who were going down the wrong road with their insurance planning and running counter to their growth pattern and the inflation cycles. They are married to each other and have been coshareholders in their business for many years. Both work and contribute equally in every respect; it is not a case of one putting the name of the other on the business door just for tax or other personal reasons. There was joint ownership not only in their business, but also in all the numerous and valuable outside landholdings they had. One of their problems was the type of investment they liked the best: they are complete devotees of investing in vacant land for resale later. Even though they both earn high incomes, there is always the risk of a serious cash shortage because of the nature of the estate: high property taxes on land that does not produce any depreciation or real income.

Even though the estate value had been growing in recent years, they had been taking cost-cutting measures in the wrong areas. The jointly owned property would result in high estate taxes someday; therefore, high liquidity would be needed. They were both enticed by the current practice of dropping term premiums, even though insurance premiums were the smallest of their budgetary drains. However, they were convinced that the falling premiums were heaven-sent, like manna. In the past three years, with their accountant's acquiescence, they had dropped a considerable amount of permanent insurance. Compounding this, they jumped on the term bandwagon and had me change their company three times in the last three years. Within the last year, they had

Illustration 9. Tell Like It Is — Agenda

BRODE, LANDSBERG, MEISEL & HAAS

V—— AND N—— ASSOCIATES

AGENDA — MAY 12, 1983

1. Life Insurance

    a) Inflation—Deflation—Joint Property

    b) Illiquid

    c) Dating

    d) Mathematics

Insured	Company	Amount	S.A. Premium	Deposit	Balance
V	Security Conn.	$ 500,000	$ 470.60	$ 470.60	—0—
N	Security Conn.	$ 500,000	917.80	904.40	$ 13.40
			$1,388.40	$1,375.00	$ 13.40
N	Security Conn.	$1,000,000	$1,710.80	$ 904.40	$806.40

2. Personal Disability

    a) Companies Analyzed—Paul Revere, Union Mutual, Monarch, Connecticut Mutual, Provident

    b) Conclusion—Loss to A's by changing; because of age and excellence of coverage

    c) Recommendation—Complete your program by buying riders and taking new allowable increased limits

3. Group Benefits

    a) Census List of Employees

4.

5.

changed both their accountant and attorney. So you see, these people are not afraid of change; they welcome it. Unfortunately, it was all on the cheap side. My position was that if I could not regain their confidence in sound advice, I did not want them as clients anymore.

This agenda, as simple as it looks, was designed to give a stern lecture. My goal was to reinstate full-time permanent insurance and to get them to abandon their opportunistic approach to estate planning. I was prepared to be fired after this meeting because I intended to be as blunt as possible regarding my role and the fact that my ideas did not fit in with what they were erroneously attempting to accomplish. If they would not take my advice, I was prepared to say that what was on this agenda was a stepping-stone for growth and if we could not go forward, rather than sideways as we had been, I did not care to continue.

I labored a very long while in my office trying to come up with a lecture I could deliver that would have the result I wanted rather than just sounding hard-nosed and losing the client because I insulted them. I felt that being sincere and honest would ring loud and be accepted by them because they knew what I was suggesting was the right thing rather than the expedient road they were now using. It was a "good news-bad news" detour, the good news being no large cash outlays now. The bad news was they would end up nowhere and someone else would spend their money trying to extricate them from the wreck. Eleven yellow legal sheets came down to what you see in item 1. I was delivering the policies you see under the section entitled, "d) Mathematics."

I decided to approach the whole problem as an offshoot of the policies now on the table. I entitled item 1 "Life Insurance." Item 1(a) allowed me to sermonize about inflation and the fact that their practice of dropping the permanent and setting up less term insurance because the premiums were a bogus bargain right now, was exactly counter to the way the economy and their estates were going. I told them I felt they had lost sight of the goals of their planning and were caught up with costs to such an extent that unless things happened in the exact order they wanted, all the planning could be worthless and the acquiring of the estate would have been only a profitable hobby while they were alive. It would be gone before their children and grandchildren had a chance to inherit it. The beneficiaries would be the insurance people and tax advisers now, and to a generous extent later, the various levels of government, which would receive an unnecessarily large amount of estate taxes.

I was able to get into the area of the joint property myth for their assets and the need for honestly accepting the advice of good tax counsel. In 1(b), I discussed the illiquid nature of the makeup of the property they owned, and the need for insurance that would be full-time, to guarantee the retention of the rest of the assets. In 1(c), I spoke of the great timing of the estate tax laws that allow the unlimited marital deduction. I also explained the downside risk that a changing of the guard in Congress could change the highly favorable tax laws now in effect.

In the math section of 1(d), I outlined the money I had to pick up for the policies on "V" and "N." This gave me the opportunity to talk about the inadequacy of these amounts in their estates. The result was excellent. They did not mind my being honest rather than diplomatic. We applied for additional coverage through their retirement plans. They felt better and so did I.

In item 2, I did an analysis for them of the possibility of changing their disabilty policies in order to get "more economical" coverage. They were approached by someone else who had used that line, not even knowing what coverage they already owned. I knew there was no way to improve on what we already had in force because the companies were the best, the definitions were the best, and the ages of issue were the best, because they were younger. I did not spend too much time analyzing the proposals for the companies listed under point 2(a), but I did show the pile of booklets that came out of asking one question. I asked if they wanted to take the propositions with them for study. This whole discussion started because of their tightwad attitude about premiums. In point 2(b), I showed them the loss they would suffer because of the advancement of age. Under this item, I also pointed out that I would be happy to make a change incorporating the old policies with the new limits into one contract with a new company that I could have promoted, just for the reason of making more commissions. However, my recommendation was summarized in point 2(c). They agreed quickly when they saw I would have been the only winner under a replacement of excellent policies with excellent companies.

Point 3 is an interesting one because I did no preparation for it. I received a phone call from one of them while the underwriting was going on for the life policies in item 1. She quizzed me on the idea of getting additional complementary coverage through the group route. Her motive was to further cut premiums. I conveyed the merits of the idea and said we could discuss it on delivery of the policies now being underwritten. My thought was not to muddy up the waters with anything other than that which is necessary to stay on point. These people had already exasperated a number of other professionals. At the time of the phone call, I was already planning my last-ditch strategy as I outlined above, and I was going to do nothing to even hint at a change of course. These new policies were to be a base for keeping them on course. Frankly, I wanted to regain control of this case. In this regard, the only thing I did on delivery was to explain the group philosophy and legal requirements, including nondiscrimination in favor of highly paid personnel. I restated the facts about the current policies being the basis for future growth and not being the target for opportunism. They agreed and I left the census blanks to be filled out.

This will complete the chapter on agendas. To summarize, I say that the agendas work for me. I enjoy writing the game plan for an interview and seeing how close to being right I can be. So far the clients are voting with me since they're buying the ideas and the products.

*   *   *

5.

"THE WHITE FOG"

I was talking with a client a few years ago concerning a paper mill strike taking place at that time. He was the owner of a print shop and he explained to me the plight of the mill owners. The net profit of the paper mill was about 1 percent, making it far more profitable for investors simply to leave the $10 million required to open a plant in the bank at the then rate of 5 percent. On the one hand, labor needed more money; on the other hand, there was just no way that the owners could afford to pay it. (As Tevye from *Fiddler on the Roof* said, "On the other hand," the world needed the paper.) I was really moved by this dilemma. Mind you, this was before the days of the kind of inflation we're now suffering, and during the days when gasoline was selling for 50 cents a gallon.

Well, that strike is over, and the world has taken a few turns since then. I'm not aware, but maybe we've had another paper strike or two; inflation engulfs us; oil prices have soared. I don't know what happened to the price of paper, but the stuff multiplies like rats, or hangers in a closet. If snow stopped coming to Michigan for a decade or two, some entrepreneur could fool the populace by merely shredding up the stuff that comes across my desk and dropping it from planes. I've got plenty. The stream never stops. Some days, I measure my productivity by the number of wastebaskets I fill. Usually, it's only one per day, but some days I sneak some out into the front secretary's office and some days I have to step into the basket to squeeze in a little more.

If anything was ever going to hurt the world's paper supply, it should have been computers, but the flow goes on. The computer did what it was supposed to do—speed up communication—but even in its voluminous vomiting of paper, in duplicate, it can't slow down the flow. The only paper shortage I've ever noticed is when the machine runs out, and that only happens when someone forgets to order another bale.

All of this brings me to the chapter title, "The White Fog." If it weren't for the desire to save paper, I would give the reader four blank pages to figure out what it's all about. In my book, "No, I Can't Afford It," I talked about "the forty-one memo syndrome" which referred to the corporate smoke screen to get something done. But an apt description of the smoke screen that blurs so much business progress is "The White Fog," which I first heard from my friend, Don Pond, of the Connecticut Mutual home office pension department.

Illustration 10 is a photo of a half-sheet of paper that I have now seen again and again in all forms of correspondence from the IRS and other government agencies. It all sounds wonderful, but it appears that it is a matter of saying it, but not doing it. To my eyes this slip of paper is merely an additional one. It talks about the Paperwork Reduction Act. It gives instructions about the rights of individuals to question or look further into the Act. As an author talking about shortening verbiage, I probably should exercise my rights and send for a copy of the Act. I'm afraid of what might come to

Illustration 10. Paperwork Reduction Act Notice

**Department of the Treasury
Internal Revenue Service**

Paperwork Reduction Act Notice

We ask for this information to carry out the Internal Revenue laws of the United States. We need it to ensure that taxpayers are complying with these laws and to allow us to figure and collect the right amount of tax. You are required to give us this information.

Notice 610 (Rev. 11-82)

U.S. G.P.O. 1983-659-068:333   23-188-5979

me in the mail. It's interesting to get this notice with some government mail. I can't find anything else missing; this thing is just there. I don't know what has been reduced; if something were missing, I don't know what it is because it isn't mentioned. All the other mail is there. Some forms of correspondence come with both an original and a copy. The copy is for the receiver to keep and the instructions are voluminous and fully confusing. It would be interesting to find out if any paper were actually reduced. There is probably no way to know and there is no way that I'm going to ask.

The insurance companies aren't much better either. Even if an agent were only writing business for one company and he or she never brokered a policy, there would still be an unending stream of paper coming to the office. If one is representing a few companies, the torrent is multiplied. Each company tries to do a good job of informing us of the changes in rates, laws, practices, underwriting, and so forth, but the compounding paperwork becomes confounding. Add to this the good intentions of the manager or general agent and the floodgates are opened. Top that off with the brokerage houses that buy lists of names of agents, then solicit our business with their "loss leaders." The banks help us out with their monthly news bulletins. Now, the accountants and lawyers have gotten into the business of outside advertising, so we get a spate of that stuff. It's amazing how much of the mail coming from these sources is exactly alike. You would like to pitch it all but you're afraid one good thing might come from somewhere in the depths of one of those circulars. So much of that material is bought from the same publishing or news service. Some of the work I do on Saturdays is trying to be selective about reading or pitching my weekly influx.

In this chapter, I'm going to discuss my attempts to cut down on the paper glut. I've accused a few parties of causing it, but I must admit that we as agents do add to it also. Some of us love the computer. It's so nice and official, usually right, and even when it's not, it rarely gets caught. It certainly is replacing the ratebook and that is a minor paper offset. One of the rules in the computer training manual regarding preparation of proposals is that there must be four variations, with carbon. And, of course, every other proposal run must have an error in it. Have you ever seen the wastebaskets of the computer operators in the agencies?

Since they are so easy to get and truly give so much information, some agents order alternate proposals by the pound, and try to sell by ingenuity of machinery. It's no wonder some prospects say, "I want to think it over." Who can absorb all that material and still appear to be a conscientious buyer, rather than saying, "yes" by intimidation only. The paper chase never ends. I abhor it and this is one of the reasons for the agenda system. Another thing I do is spend my Saturday mornings preparing cases. In that preparation, I do the diet training for my proposals. I'm going to demonstrate some of these in later chapters. In this chapter, I'm going to show the basic one I developed for term-permanent illustrations. I did show this one in previous books, but it is a mainstay of more complex ones developed since, so in order to show those in another chapter, I must lay the groundwork. My purpose with these stripped-down illustrations is to present the one-word, one-thought type of interviews that I mentioned. At the interviews the dialogue is important, but my desire is to keep the attention focused on what is *most* important and not on the mental sparring of preplanning objections and dodges. For the purists, full disclosure of dividends and other legal requirements are a part of each interview. If I asked clients whether they wanted the full four pounds of paper or only what is important, the answer would always be, "Just tell me the facts, ma'am." To you, I say, "Follow the bouncing ball."

About 10 years ago, I gave up the use of the words "term" and "permanent" to illustrate insurance policies. I realized that there were too many preconceptions that went with the words. On some occasions, if I showed a permanent policy only, questions concerning term insurance would be asked. Then, no matter how erudite my language might be, I found that the client had to defend his ideas against mine. No matter what I said, I was backtracking. If the client started to agree with me, it was easy and even reasonable for him to say, "Let's start with the term, and I'll change later." Now, where this is the right solution, I have no quarrel with the idea and probably will be the one to suggest it.

I reasoned, was it really the name of the policy we were selling, or was it what the policy would do? The vital statistics were face amount, premium, and cash value. If we never tell the prospect the name of the plan, how can he or she object to the idea that does him the most good, no matter what it is called? Our actuaries and marketing committees are great. I've made my share of actuary jokes, but I legitimately admire and respect our "numbers" men and women. I trust them when I quote a rate. I have no way of making the calculations, and I find it very convenient to go to a ratebook or to a machine and get a quote.

I know every insurance plan must have a name—the state insurance departments require it—but if we looked in the Flitcraft and started a list of 100 names, we'd be astounded by the poetry that goes into a financial package called a policy. When we give it serious thought, we as agents truly are to be complimented for explaining the attributes of some of the fancy acronyms we use for policies. Sometimes, it's no wonder that the prospect says he wants to think it over; he doesn't understand what names like "President's Eagle Whole Life" or "Centennial Select Permanent" or "Recontrovertible Competitor" mean. He isn't dumb, but he might appear so if he accepted all the fancy prose we use without even questioning it.

With the intent of getting rid of the unnecessary verbiage and distractions, I decided to eliminate, almost completely, the names of plans. We all know, once we firmly establish the need and excite the client about solving the problem, that the only thing left to focus on is the consideration, fee price, payment, or to use that marvelously descriptive word, the *Premium*. This evaluation led to illustration 11, which has become the basis for most of my closes in the last few years. Let me remind you of *the* most important thing. Don't close until there is a need. Only then do I present alternatives to accommodate the need.

In illustration 11, the need was $150,000 of key-person insurance on the son of a long-time client. The boy had just graduated from college and was entering his dad's business. The $150,000 amount was arrived at to coincide with the intended value of the stock Bob would receive as a gift from his father in the next few years. The insurance was to be a key-man asset now, then switched to a stock-redemption format when necessary. In effect, it was a future option sale.

Frank, the father, was one of the policyowners with whom I had grown. His first policy, in 1957, had a $7,000 face amount; now the premiums are triple that. The need was firmly fixed, so the purpose now was to place the best-suited policy. I felt that stringing the whole 44 years to age 65 would be very effective in showing the progression, or regression, of premiums. The first two columns are self-explanatory. The third column shows premiums for five-year renewable term. That's what we were showing a few years ago; on average, the premiums beat yearly renewable term, at that time. Presently, we know it is a whole new ball game in the term field, and I will be showing some illustrations on that basis; however, this proposal is shown exactly as it was then. The fourth column illustrates a policy that consists of about 70 percent permanent as basic insurance, and about 30 percent term, which automatically converts itself within the policy by use of dividends, so that it always remains at the full face amount. Some companies call these contracts "Extraordinary Life" or "Enhancement." The fourth column could also be used to show nonparticipating insurance. The fifth column shows participating permanent insurance with dividends used to reduce premiums.

Illustration 11. Term vs. Permanent

TERM VS. PERMANENT

AGE 21		BOB _____		$150,000
YEAR	AGE	INCREASING PREMIUM	LEVEL PREMIUM	DECREASING PREMIUM
1	21	$ 499.50	$ 1,152.00	$ 1,902.00
2	22	499.50	1,152.00	1,902.00
3	23	499.50	1,152.00	1,777.50
4	24	499.50	1,152.00	1,677.00
5	25	499.50	1,152.00	1,587.00
6	26	504.00	1,152.00	1,501.50
7	27	504.00	1,152.00	1,423.50
8	28	504.00	1,152.00	1,354.50
9	29	504.00	1,152.00	1,293.50
10	30	504.00	1,152.00	1,242.00
11	31	531.00	1,152.00	1,188.00
12	32	531.00	1,152.00	1,134.00
13	33	531.00	1,152.00	1,078.50
14	34	531.00	1,152.00	1,029.00
15	35	531.00	1,152.00	1,011.00
16	36	628.50	1,152.00	940.50
17	37	628.50	1,152.00	894.00
18	38	628.50	1,152.00	847.50
19	39	628.50	1,152.00	814.50
20	40	628.50	1,152.00	778.50
21	41	828.00	1,152.00	742.50
22	42	828.00	1,152.00	714.00
23	43	828.00	1,152.00	684.00
24	44	828.00	1,152.00	655.50
25	45	828.00	1,152.00	625.50
26	46	1,179.00	1,152.00	592.50
27	47	1,179.00	1,152.00	562.50
28	48	1,179.00	1,152.00	529.50
29	49	1,179.00	1,152.00	496.50
30	50	1,179.00	1,152.00	463.50
31	51	1,752.00	1,152.00	432.00
32	52	1,752.00	1,152.00	396.00
33	53	1,752.00	1,152.00	364.50
34	54	1,752.00	1,152.00	330.00
35	55	1,752.00	1,152.00	297.00
36	56	2,572.50	1,152.00	262.50
37	57	2,572.50	1,152.00	226.50
38	58	2,572.50	1,152.00	190.50
39	59	2,572.50	1,152.00	156.00
40	60	2,572.50	1,152.00	120.00
41	61	4,182.00	1,152.00	85.50
42	62	4,182.00	1,152.00	51.00
43	63	4,182.00	1,152.00	16.50
44	64	4,182.00	1,152.00	18.00 (CR)
TOTALS @ 65		$59,605.50	$50,688.00	$34,324.50
CASH VALUES @ 65		-0-	$89,095.00	$85,800.00

When we finished establishing the problem and the solution, I showed this abridged illustration. I explained to father and son that there were three kinds of policies to solve the needs: Increasing Premium, Level Premium, or Decreasing Premium. The Increasing Premium starts at a low of $499.50 at age 21 and reaches a high of $4,182.00 at age 65. The total premiums to age 65 would be $59,605.50, and the cash value would be zero. The Level Premium starts at $1,152.00 and remains constant. By age 65, the total premium would be $50,688.00, and the cash value would be $89,095.00. The Decreasing Premium plan starts at a high of $1,902.00 and decreases to a point at age 65, whereby the insurance company will be paying Bob $18 to keep the policy. The total premium would be $34,324.50 and holding, and the cash value would be $85,800.00. Using this kind of display makes it tough to get out the words saying, "We'll take the Increasing Premium."

The father did have a few questions and they were leading toward the Increasing Premium. I was about to start answering when the son said, "Dad, I can picture myself being your age of 47. Look at the sheet. By 47, we would be paying $1,179 under the increasing and only $562.50 under the decreasing." Notice he skipped the Level Premium in the center column. Apparently the illustration had made its point, since the discussion was steering toward what I felt was the best policy, Decreasing Premium, Permanent. Also, at this point, I was not doing any selling; young Bob was telling his father all the obvious pluses.

As an aside, I should point out that this was rather unique and, since that time, I have learned to place the plan I want to sell in the center column, if I'm showing three choices. With two choices, I have found that placing the desired policy second works best. I don't know the psychology behind all of this. People generally feel better in the middle, they don't like their flanks exposed. In the two-choice illustration, just like the department store, people don't like to buy the first thing they are shown.

In the interview, we were now down to a discussion between "increasing" or "decreasing." The father responded by saying, "The Decreasing costs four times as much to start." Bob replied, "But, Dad, you told me this corporation never rents anything, we only buy our machinery. We never get anything back with the Increasing. We make a $51,000 gain with the Decreasing. It seems like we're only leasing the insurance and paying too much." I was thinking to myself that I could not have said it any better, so I kept silent. Dad said, "You're right, Bob. Burt, we'll take the Decreasing."

This has been the predominant reasoning since I started using this kind of proposal. The logic of the presentation was just summed up beautifully by a 21-year-old budding executive. Since that time, I have very rarely used the words "term" or "permanent" or any of their pseudonyms. I have developed many variations of this main theme, and I will show some of these in the chapters following.

This is a good spot to demonstrate illustration 12. It portrays one of the principles I spoke about in illustration 11. The special point I made there was to place the plan you were desirous of selling in the center column. This illustration does just that. The background developed with a phone call from a client who said he wanted to buy $100,000 of term insurance for his wife. I said I would draw a plan for them and we made an appointment for the three of us. I figured the case out as follows: first, I don't want to sell term insurance since it is not the right thing for this client. Second, we could have a great debate since it was he who called me and placed an order. I had to suspect that some other agent had gotten to one of them, or perhaps, he had simply read something about wife insurance. Third, I was not going to use the words "term" or "permanent," even though he had already brought one of them out into the open. Fourth, I was going to use the illustration format that you have just seen in illustration 11; after all, that is why I develop these things, so that I will never have to duplicate time spent brainstorming a case

Illustration 12. One-Word Close

ROSIE

$100,000 coverage (including waiver of premium)

Beginning Policy Year	Increasing Premium (No Equity)	Increasing Premium (Enriched Equity)	Increasing Premium (With Equity)
1	$ 256	$ 1,034	$ 429
2	277	1,053	434
3	303	1,086	562
4	329	1,120	706
5	361	1,149	852
6	393	1,177	997
7	433	1,202	1,134
8	475	1,223	1,266
9	525	1,245	1,399
10	588	1,266	1,528
11	658	1,283	1,650
12	744	1,296	1,771
13	834	1,306	1,888
14	919	1,308	1,993
15	1,015	1,307	2,092
16	1,129	1,302	2,188
17	924	1,291	2,073
18	953	1,280	1,960
19	977	1,267	1,849
20	901	1,254	1,740
20 Years Premiums	$12,285	$22,633	$26,681
20th-Year Equity	- 0 -	$29,222	$27,387
20th-Year Free Continuing Coverage	- 0 -	$47,500	$46,900

that falls into a pattern situation. Fifth, Rosie was a pretty classy lady and the better quality product will always appeal to her. The same was true for Bill, but he might like to win the "term" argument no matter how good the alternative is.

I did not spend too much time figuring out what I would do. The result of my meeting with myself is as you see it in illustration 12. The first column is the policy year. The second shows the annual renewable term. Column 3, which is the one I wanted to place, is 20-Year Graded Premium Life. Column 4 is 15-Year Graded Premium Life. I decided to give them three choices instead of two, since I was now appealing to Rosie's sense of shopping expertise. Relating to premium, the significant thing about all of these plans is that they all have increasing premiums, not only the term in the first column. What then distinguishes the Graded Premium Life (GPL) from the term? The answer is the cash value. So, it became a simple thing to differentiate the two types by just referring to the "equity" or "nonequity" basis.

Both the GPL 15 and the GPL 20 have equities. The GPL 20 is the better buy in 20 years, but the GPL 15 has a cash value also, and it costs less for the first seven years. I was going to be present at this interview so I could explain all these things, but my object with these types of displays is to make the prospects select their own plan and then reaffirm out loud what their minds have already decided. The GPL 20 is the best net cost buy, but it takes time to develop the interview to interject that thought. The interview would not be a long, complicated one in any event, but I try to sell my inventions at the earliest possible moment. It appeared to me that the key were the references to "Equity." Therefore, I had to think of a word that would make the GPL 20 seem like the obvious quality choice. The reference to a one-word close on this proposal is answered by the word "Enriched" in the fourth column.

I guess I did it right. Their eyes focused in on the key word and every point they made had to do with the better ultimate results of plan two. I only had to sit and agree. From their vantage point, I don't think it came across as a sales situation. It was a simple matter of selecting the product that suited them best. They never brought up the subject of the first phone call, which was about term insurance. For sure, I wasn't going to do it. This is not unusual and it was the first point I made regarding generic titles.

Another benefit of this type of spreadsheet is the fact that a string of premiums appears. I sense that too often agents get trapped in the cost debate because the term premium for the first year comes across so low in comparison with the first-year permanent premium, and takes a good sales effort after that to grab the prospect's full attention in order to explain all the facts. Consider this: A newspaper headline may only consist of three words: "Joe Sues Burt." Now, everyone thinks that I did something wrong. After all the paper would not print anything wrong, would it? My defense either in the paper or in court could be brilliant. I can win the case; I can demolish the accusers. I can prove there never was anything to their case. I can even launch a countersuit. But in the minds of some there will always be that lingering doubt. If we let the term argument get too much of a foothold, the situation is much the same. He who fires the first shot usually holds the advantageous position.

*   *   *

6.

WHO SAYS SO?

As we said in Chapter One, the purpose of the children's game, Simon Says, is to eliminate all players except one. The essence of the game is to give instructions for movements. The leader of the moment gives the instructions and the other players first respond, "May I?" The leader then has the option of saying "yes" or "no." The key to the game is the phrase, "May I." The orders can be given with varying degrees of speed or enthusiasm, all with the goal of getting the other players to make the movements without the key words. Anxiousness usually gets the better of the participants, and a whole lot of movement occurs without the question. All kinds of trickery are allowed with the leader's object to keep the other players from crossing a certain line by confusing them.

Salespeople do a lot of that too. Almost all the time it is done unwittingly, but we do force our buyers to say, "May I?" on occasion. We do this by presenting too much paper and too much dialogue. The object is to sell, but not to tell everything we know about every situation to every prospect. I submit that we tell too much. When the prospects are ready to buy, let them. When all the signals are there no matter how far it is into the interview, start closing the sale. I think by now you are aware that my purpose is to let the prospect buy as early as possible but to shorten the talking time and highlight the viewing material. Look at illustration 13 as an instance of using one illustration for more than one purpose and for reaffirmation of that purpose in protecting against dying too soon or living too long.

At the lower right of illustration 13, you will notice the date October 1980. I had sold this case during the football season. Since 1964, Sharon and I have been attending Michigan State football games. At a tailgate party, my daughter, Shelley, told me that her economics professor said, "Never buy whole life. The agent only sells it because he makes more commissions." I was and still am furious to think that a college teacher is telling this to 300 19- to 20-year-old college students each day. I asked if this professor ever allowed guest lecturers. Shelley told me that he did. I asked her to ask him if he wanted to have an easy day.

A couple of weeks later I asked her if he had responded to her question and she said she had had difficulty talking to him because he was always in a hurry to leave the lecture hall promptly at 9:50 A.M. when the class ended. I asked why he was in such a rush to leave and she told me he had to hurry for the market opening since he was a stockbroker. I asked her to persist in getting the question to him. She finally made contact and he said he would think about working it out later in the year. He stalled and he dodged and we never had the meeting. I even wrote to the university president who, following channels, got this guy to respond to my letter. He wrote to the dean saying his class is not Sesame Street; however, if he could make time, he would have me in. He evaded me and we never got together.

In spite of the fact that I had no date, I started getting ready for this speech. I am the same age as the client in illustration 13, so I just put my name on a photocopy of the il-

Illustration 13. Cutting Class

BURT MEISEL

$1,000,000 OF PROTECTION   AGE: 48

Year	Increasing Premium		Increasing Premium (With Equity)		Decreasing Premium (With Equity)	
1	$ 7,280	*3,640*	$ 13,885	*6,942*	$ 26,720	*13,360*
2	7,930	*634*	14,870	*2,360*	25,190	*3,326*
3	8,710	*697*	15,395	*2,527*	24,630	*3,326*
4	9,420	*466*	15,935	*1,860*	24,100	*1,870*
5	10,340	*512*	16,505	*2,058*	23,570	*1,870*
6	11,360	*563*	17,065	*2,053*	23,020	*1,870*
7	12,430	*616*	17,615	*2,151*	22,710	*1,870*
8	13,540	*335*	18,145	*1,138*	22,420	*534*
9	14,740	*364*	18,655	*1,165*	21,790	*534*
10	15,960	*394*	19,155	*1,188*	21,030	*534*
11	17,390	*429*	19,655	*1,221*	20,280	*534*
12	19,190	*472*	20,115	*1,249*	19,540	*534*
13	21,630	*527*	20,535	*1,276*	18,830	*534*
14	24,150	*583*	20,935	*1,304*	18,120	*534*
15	26,580	*641*	21,375	*1,332*	17,210	*534*
16	29,060	*704*	21,785	*1,359*	16,330	*534*
17	31,560	*757*	22,185	*1,387*	15,480	*534*
18	34,410	*826*	22,545	*1,415*	14,670	*534*
19	37,240	*890*	22,915	*1,443*	13,900	*534*
20	40,410	*965*	23,085	*1,471*	12,680	*534*
21	44,080	*1,048*	23,215	*1,499*	11,540	*534*
22	48,560	*1,147*	21,935	*832*	10,480	*534*
23	54,130	*1,266*	20,315	*832*	9,460	*534*
24	59,900	*1,391*	19,035	*832*	8,510	*534*
25	66,220	*1,525*	17,925	*832*	7,470	*534*
Total Premium	$791,570	*20,126*	$484,785	*38,726*	$449,690	*37,111*
Total Equity	— 0 —		$467,950		$553,870	
Total Continuing Coverage— No Premium	— 0 —		$608,000		$732,000	

Dividends are based on the current dividend scale and are not guaranteed

October 1980

lustration I had recently sold. If you will concentrate on the block-typewritten part of the illustration and not pay attention to the italicized part (originally handwritten), you will see that it is the same type of three-column proposal we have been examining. The first plan shown is term and I labeled it as "Increasing Premium." The second column is GPL 20, and I labeled it as "Increasing Premium (With Equity)." The third plan shown is ordinary life with dividends used to reduce the premium; I called this one "Decreasing Premium (With Equity)." (Incidentally, the proposal worked and the client selected the center column as the one for his corporation.)

I used the same illustration that I had just used for the sale and took the time to calculate the commissions from age 48 to 73 on all these plans. These calculations turn up as the italicized (handwritten) numbers right next to all the block-typed columns. As it turned out, the teacher was right in one respect; on both ordinary life plans, if I live and my client lives to expectancy, I earn either $38,726 or $37,111, as opposed to $20,126 on a term sale.

In the same period, on the term basis, the client would have paid $791,570 to have zero equity. On the GPL 20, he would have paid $484,785 to have an equity of $467,950. Let us not even take into consideration the decreasing premium plan. Getting back to the GPL 20 as compared to the term, I would have asked the professor, and I pose the question to anyone, am I worth $18,000 more commissions for a spread of approximately an $800,000 difference.? Isn't anyone in this world worth a fee of $18,000 more for making a $467,000 pot of cash as opposed to a $791,000 cost? If this isn't a better use of money, I would have beseeched the professor to show me what was. I don't care what kind of math is used or how the figures are manipulated: on the one hand, there is some money; on the other, there is only cost.

I'm sorry I never got to use that illustration for the students at the college. The numbers themselves are revealing but there is another factor here. That is the ongoing use of a simple illustration. It really was no hard job at all to take the three-column proposal that I use for selling insurance and turn it to another use. That is something I try to do with all my proposals: make them so they are universal and can fit more than one situation. After all, the whole world of insurance is only built on two theories: the law of large numbers and the law of compound interest. The variations never stop, but the basic principles are truly simple. The criticisms of our product never stop, but they too are built on a couple of simple objections that can be answered with simple, but thought-provoking demonstrations.

As an aside to the main issue here, I point out the use of the words "Continuing Coverage" instead of "Paid-Up Insurance."

Illustration 14 is very interesting. Here, the use of key words completely sells the case, and the onus is taken off the policy with the lowest first-year premium. The background of the case is as follows. RNL is already a client both on a personal and corporate basis. He has purchased both permanent and term insurance for differing needs. The policies were all from the Connecticut Mutual Insurance Co. We were preparing to do considerably more planning and insurance increases when I received a phone call from him stating that he had heard from a friend about a very low-cost term policy from another company, and he wondered why I had not shown him this policy for his term needs. This is not an unusual question these days in the era of the "low-cost term."

My question is "low cost for how long"? We have all been snookered into this type of comparison. In fact, sometimes when I'm questioned regarding the lowest term policies, I respond by asking what day it is. I then relay to the asker that I will quote the rates that I had as of last weekend, but also relay that I have not yet opened my mail this morning. In spite of the fact that some of us have taken to the tactic of churning out term policies, we have adopted a practice of the

Illustration 14. A Rose By Any Other Name

BRODE, LANDSBERG, MEISEL & HAAS

RNL

$250,000 PROTECTION

	(SWAN) SN	(COUTURIER) CONN. MUTUAL
1983	$ 407.50	$ 477.50
1984	547.50	580.00
1985	672.50	700.00
1986	825.00	747.50
1987	990.00	792.50
1988	1,267.50	805.00
1989	1,547.50	872.50
	$6,257.50	$4,975.00

APRIL 1983

Dividends Not Guaranteed

stockbrokers. They are in contact with their clients every day by phone. Their products change in price with every tick of the tape. Ours are not that bad, but it is tough to keep up with the "bargains" that come in with the mailman. All of them advertise the lowest rates, but they only last till the 2 P.M. delivery.

Some of us get panicky and fall into the trap of accepting the hype as correct, even though we really know that the client would be better off with a policy from a large, solid, old-line company that has a good portfolio of both term contracts and ordinary products. Some of the rate toutsheets that come through my office are phenomenally low for the first year and could excite anyone, agents included, if that were the only factor being considered. No policy in the world should be judged on just one year's projections unless it is designed for one year only and the express intention is to terminate it after that period. Then the lowest rate on the street should be "considered." I say "considered" because there are still other factors besides the premium, even if it is intended to be a 365-day, stop-order sale. I am still concerned about the reserves and reputation of the company. One might say I am taking a conservative scare position, but even though the premium is low, $500,000 is a lot of money, and I still want a semblance of certainty that the claim will be paid.

No one should ever consider a program of ongoing insurance by only evaluating the first-year premium. When a person buys a house or a car, he or she also weighs the costs of upkeep, taxes, and so on. Even if the intention is to keep the term policy for a very short period, if the insured should become disabled or uninsurable, and a conversion must take place, I feel the full-time permanent policy should be a good one. Otherwise, the term policy was the worst investment of premiums that was ever made and the agent will bear the brunt of the insured's scorn even if the instructions were to get the "cheapest" coverage possible. (The finger-pointing, fast-talking, and excuse-making don't balance off the expedient cost for the client and the commission for the agent at the time of the "real" payment.) With that in mind, I always show the term of my parent company, Connecticut Mutual. I might have to follow orders and get comparative quotes from the specialty companies, but my first inclination is for quality.

Since I was asked to defend my past actions and still make recommendations for my client, I decided to do it in the language that meant the most to him. I have used the format in illustration 14 many times in the past. On the one side, I list the low-ball premium and on the other I list the quality company. Too often, we face the situation of short-sightedness or hasty decisions based on preconceptions or extraneous information. Too often we can't even get the words out of our mouths fast enough before the prospect either tells us about the plan he or she heard of or selects the cheapest first-year premium. Now that doesn't make much sense in a case where the ultimate policy will be whole life. What difference does one, two, or three premiums make in a 30-year program with the last 27 of them being a permanent program? If the client is going to be angry, I think the ire will be greater if he or she compares the results of an inferior whole-life policy 10 or 20 years after it is in force, as opposed to $70 more premium for the first year. But the key ingredient is not to let a negative attitude toward the quality product creep in before you have had a chance to give a full presentation. What we must get is a chance at full disclosure. After all, that is what the clients and the IRS are telling us they want.

Remember, I was on the defensive in this interview because the phone call came to me after the client became aware of a "cheaper" premium than the last quarter-million policy I had sold him. There was a considerable amount of insurance under consideration for the newly updated stock-redemption agreement and I found myself under fire a little bit. I thought about it for a long while and resolved to myself that the difference was simply "cheap" versus "quality." I reasoned that all my clients had this sort of problem; it was not unique to me. All of them have one product that is superior to another that is available. This particular business was an eyeglass frame supplier. I called the company and asked someone I know, "What is the best frame you have?" The answer was "Couturier." "What is the lowest priced?" I asked. Response: "Swan, but we don't carry it."

Now look again at illustration 14 and if you know what is coming before you look, move on to illustration 15. I did a display of the two companies "SN" and "Connecticut Mutual." Over the names of the insurance companies, I put "(Swan)" and "(Couturier)." I promise you that I said very few words after putting the paper in front of "RNL." He said everything for me. He took the time to look at the whole illustration before he spoke, whereupon he said, "I would put $1,300 more into the 'Swan' policy." I summoned up my best cowboy drawl and responded, "Yup." He said, "The 'Couturier' is less after only three years." "Yup." I answered, "We don't want that kind of cost for just seven years," he stated. I said, "OK."

The sale was considerably larger than that which is shown here. I was only using this one because I had recently placed a similar policy with him. I did not have to illustrate the larger sale; they simply told me the face amounts and I said, "Yup." The date of that interview is shown at the lower right as April 1983. Since then I have used this format whenever I have to illustrate a strictly term proposal. For example, I just completed a transaction with a manufacturer who told me about fiberglass linings competing unfairly with the quality of steel. You know exactly how my illustration to him came out in order to put the competitive edge on my side. The competition might say I stole this case with my "(Steel)" proposal. Think about your clients' businesses when you prepare a case. If you don't know the generic item from the high-priced spread, make a phone call to the business. Two things will happen on the appointment: your client will be curious to see the differences in products instead of just the first-year "loss leader" cost, and he will appreciate your sales ability because he is out in the market fighting the same battle you are with the same labels attached.

It is apparent that all my efforts are toward a shorthand of words and especially paper. I can think of an example of an entire profession that does this better than any other. Most doctors probably see six to eight patients an hour and some see considerably more. That is a tremendous number of case histories. It's rare that the doctor comes into the examining room and says, "Now let's see, what's the problem?" That line is saved for the brand new patient. If he has seen you before, he walks into the room with both lips still smoking from talking to the last patient. You better believe, with that number of patients, he doesn't remember your little hurts and unusual symptoms. In the four seconds that it takes for him to pick up your chart from the holder on the door until he is standing in front of you, he has caught up on everything that went on six months ago. He starts right in with, "You still taking your blood pressure medicine?" Then the talking is up to you, and while you try to be civil and pass a fast pleasantry, he's reading the rest of the history and catching up. I really admire their shorthand note system that enables them to have that kind of efficient time control. While I'm on the subject of time control, I wish they would use some of the saved time to answer more quickly the APSs (Attending Physician's Statement) we send them on the very same people.

Further concentrating on simplicity, take a look at illustration 15. I won't bother to give it a name. You blaspheme it with your own favorite. However, I must once again give away the credit. This succinct form is not my doing; it is one of those jokes that was given to me by a friend.

Continuing with the idea of simple, direct, straight talk, I show you a copy of a letter that I received from a very close friend and policyholder. One thing I try to stay away from is long letters, but once in a while all of us have to take wordy steps. In the case of a tough subject that has to be addressed,

Illustration 15.

Simplified 1040

Latest Revision for:

1040 Federal Income
Tax Form
Department of the Internal Revenue Service

1982
07

Your Social Security Number

PART I   INCOME

1. How much money did
   you make last year? . . . . ▶

2. Send it in . . . . ▶

I try to get to the heart of the matter, most times without the services of my secretary who is busy with her ongoing duties and underwriting work. Whenever possible, I respond to mail requests with my own handwriting right on a copy of the correspondence that came in. This does a couple of things: first, it saves time because you can respond immediately, in less time than you would use to dictate a letter. Secondly, the receiver knows that you did this work personally. Even if your handwriting isn't the prettiest, it's still yours and it has value.

In this case, Sid is a fine client whose business and personal affairs are both large and complicated. We have done a tremendous amount of planning with a huge corps of advisors through many years. His planning is excellent and up-to-date. His large insurance needs are taken care of with the proper mix of term policies and permanent policies. He called me one day to say that he had received a conversion letter for his GI insurance. Frankly, this $10,000 policy was so small a part of his total estate that I did not even include it on his last insurance summary sheet. He told me he had read the rate booklet they had sent and the term rates looked very attractive. I told him that he could not convert this term policy to another term policy. He argued with me and said he had the letter right in front of him. I told him to mail me the packet and I would examine it.

When I read the letter, I saw quickly that the whole thrust was a conversion to ordinary and not term. Rather than call Sid and spend a lot of time on the phone, or write a long letter explaining a tough concept to swallow, I decided to mark up his own letter and send it back to him. The fingers you see come from a rubber stamp we had made a few years ago. It's great for highlighting points in a document. When I want to highlight a negative point, I use a red stamp pad; otherwise, I just use black. I suppose we could use all the guile we learned in kindergarten by buying a green stamp pad but we just have not done it yet. Sometimes, I simply put the finger somewhere in the body of a letter that I think is too

Illustration 16. Term Ultimatum

Veterans Administration

MAY 2, 1983

•
S

LANSING MI 48909

Regional Office and Insurance Center
P O BOX 8079
PHILADELPHIA, PA 19101

In Reply Refer To: 310/292
FRS
W

Dear Policyholder:

YOUR "W" TERM POLICY CANNOT BE RENEWED AFTER YOUR 50TH BIRTHDAY. ALL PROTECTION UNDER THIS POLICY WILL CEASE NEXT YEAR AT THE END OF YOUR CURRENT FIVE-YEAR RENEWAL PERIOD UNLESS YOU CONVERT TO A PERMANENT PLAN OF INSURANCE.

To convert your insurance, complete the application printed on the back of this letter and send it to us with your payment for at least one monthly premium on the plan you select. You should continue to send premiums for your newly selected plan while we process your application. When approved, you will receive your new policy and premium notices.

A premium payment will not be required if your present premium is now being paid by deduction from your monthly VA pension or compensation check, allotment from active service pay or military service retirement pay. We will take action to adjust your insurance deduction to pay premiums at the new rate when we receive your conversion application.

The enclosed pamphlet describes the plans of insurance that are available to you and their premium rates. While the premium rates for the various permanent plans are somewhat higher than the premiums

(continued ...)

- 2 -

you are now paying, please keep in mind that, unlike
your term insurance, the premiums on your new permanent plan will never increase. These permanent
plans of protection also have cash, loan, paid-up
and extended insurance values and participate in
dividends.

You, of course, have the right to retain the entire amount of your insurance coverage when you
convert to a permanent plan. If you wish to keep
premium   low, however, you can elect to reduce   unt of your coverage when you convert.
If,   reading our pamphlet, you have any questions, send them to us. We will be glad to send
you additional information.

IF YOU WISH TO RETAIN YOUR VALUABLE GOVERNMENT
LIFE INSURANCE, PLEASE ACT TODAY BY SENDING US
YOUR APPLICATION AND FIRST PREMIUM PAYMENT.

VETERANS ADMINISTRATION

Enclosure

long or complicated. I throw it in there about halfway, without explanation and without regard for where it is pointing. I find that the brain, seeing a natural resting place, will gear up for a two-pronged effort on the project of reading a letter. It will also wonder why the arrow is there and read a little more slowly and intently. This way I try to make an effective impression concerning my subject.

In this letter, the key subjects were term or perm, so that's where I put the arrows or fingers. This shows the point of concentration better than anything else. Then, I penned in a message that is true not only of this GI insurance, but of all term insurance. I'm going to save this letter as a sales aid for the right moment so that it will serve its purpose regarding the choice of the two products. I think the message was pretty direct and summarizes the term syndrome. In case you can't read my writing, it says, *"Sid, I knew you when you were a young boy. This is the story of life: Time marches on. You can't have term with the Vets any more. That's the term story: it runs out—one way—or another.* (signed) *IBM.*

I find it very effective to take an existing piece of material and use it to substantiate my point or present the opposite viewpoint. Then, I can mark it up with my current comments. This way the reader can have the official source side and mine too, both in one place.

Let's go back to the chapter's title, "Who Says So?" Concentrate your attention on illustration 17, and I'll point out the most complex display I have made in a long time. This is about as detailed as I can get, but I had a reason for it and the ultimate format gave me a good prototype for the future. In this case, I was dealing with a corporation whose business was in discount health and beauty aids. There were three shareholders who owned 75 percent, 15 percent, and 10 percent, respectively. They were already dealing with another agent who was a friend of one of them. There was some group insurance in force and some personal insurance, but no

Illustration 17. Three On One

TEP — $1,000,000 STOCK REDEMPTION — NO-EQUITY PLANS

	Budget Plan	Financed Plan	
	Premium	Premium	Protection
1983	$ 1,717.20	$10,162	$1,000,000
1984	2,057.95	10,438	1,000,000
1985	2,431.73	10,846	1,000,000
1986	2,831.20	11,259	1,000,000
1987	3,263.10	0	988,365
1988	3,738.53	464	976,379
1989	4,308.66	944	964,060
1990	4,911.30	0	950,019
1991	5,593.03	0	935,135
1992	6,339.98	0	919,392
1993	7,198.50	893	903,679
1994	8,241.08	2,787	889,046
1995	9,429.73	2,741	873,623
1996	10,654.43	2,674	857,428
1997	12,006.08	2,617	840,476
1998	13,464.28	2,556	822,759
1999	11,397.45	2,495	804,295
2000	12,562.58	2,437	785,073
2001	13,879.31	2,390	765,090
2002	15,319.98	2,360	744,342
2003	17,153.38	2,312	722,822
2004	18,618.28	493	701,497
2005	20,312.48	269	680,476
2006	21,486.63	183	659,773
2007	23,506.98	149	639,456
2008	25,915.68	125	619,552
2009	28,455.63	92	600,082
2010	32,215.01	11	581,014
2011	34,764.90	0	562,488
2012	37,500.45	0	544,343
Total	$411,275.52	$71,697	

Illustration 17 (continued)

TEP — $1,000,000 STOCK REDEMPTION — WITH EQUITY PLANS

	Designer Plan			Department Store Plan		
	Premium	Equity	Protection	Premium	Equity	Protection
1983	$ 10,162	$ 957	$1,000,957	$ 10,162	$ 957	$1,000,000
1984	10,438	8,064	1,008,064	10,438	8,064	1,000,000
1985	10,846	16,077	1,016,077	10,846	16,077	1,000,000
1986	11,259	25,030	1,025,030	11,259	25,030	1,000,000
1987	11,635	33,987	1,022,352	11,635	33,987	1,000,000
1988	12,917	44,998	1,021,377	12,917	43,834	1,000,000
1989	14,209	58,249	1,022,309	14,209	54,606	1,000,000
1990	15,479	73,734	1,023,753	15,479	66,133	1,000,000
1991	16,884	91,881	1,027,016	16,884	78,522	1,000,000
1992	18,339	97,220	1,016,612	18,339	91,782	1,000,000
1993	19,831	111,467	1,015,146	19,831	105,999	1,000,000
1994	21,274	138,340	1,027,386	21,274	121,230	1,000,000
1995	22,603	168,828	1,042,451	22,603	137,370	1,000,000
1996	23,925	203,230	1,060,658	23,925	154,368	1,000,000
1997	25,272	241,910	1,082,386	25,272	172,210	1,000,000
1998	26,665	285,317	1,108,076	26,665	190,923	1,000,000
1999	28,050	333,859	1,138,154	28,050	210,455	1,000,000
2000	29,487	388,064	1,173,137	29,487	230,827	1,000,000
2001	30,972	448,482	1,213,572	30,972	252,030	1,000,000
2002	32,505	515,775	1,260,117	32,505	274,107	1,000,000
2003	34,058	590,616	1,313,438	34,058	297,069	1,000,000
2004	32,906	673,190	1,374,687	32,906	320,168	1,000,000
2005	33,231	763,245	1,443,721	33,231	342,969	1,000,000
2006	33,667	861,876	1,521,649	33,667	365,550	1,000,000
2007	34,076	1,019,854	1,659,310	34,076	387,841	1,000,000
2008	34,452	1,088,076	1,707,628	34,452	409,817	1,000,000
2009	34,780	1,217,520	1,817,602	34,780	431,444	1,000,000
2010	35,076	1,359,198	1,940,212	35,076	452,615	1,000,000
2011	35,286	1,514,503	2,076,991	35,286	473,511	1,000,000
2012	35,646	1,684,843	2,229,186	35,646	494,186	1,000,000
Total	$735,930			$735,930		

corporate planning. I had to anticipate some competition before the case was over. I also had to anticipate that the competition would bring in a Universal Life proposal as the "best" product.

I was given data that the business was worth $1 million and I used that as a basis for calculations even if it changed later on. It would be simple enough to change my quotes by applying percentages. I wanted to protect myself against low-premium term competition and floating equity competition, so I wanted to present a wide variety of plans for them to look at. When you look at the illustration, you will see the column for the years listed twice. The reason for that is that originally this illustration was in two parts. I first wanted to show term and minimum deposit plans. If you will take a piece of paper and cover up either half of the sheet right before or after the second column starting "1983," you will see what the first half of the proposal looked like alone, and then when you do the opposite you will see what the second half looked like.

To clarify what I just explained, I had two sheets, one of which contained what I called "No Equity" plans. These were "BUDGET" (term), and "FINANCED" (minimum deposit—GPL20), as one sheet. Then there was another sheet that I labeled "WITH EQUITY," consisting of "DESIGN-ER" (ordinary—GPL20) and "DEPARTMENT STORE" (ordinary—GPL20). My reasoning was to take the attention away from the names of plans as they are in the ratebook and use phrases that mean something in the jargon of the clients. "FINANCED" certainly denotes low cost early and higher cost later and that's what the term did, taking premiums totalling $411,275.52 and returning no equity. "FINANCED" was a term I dreamed up to mean minimum deposit and I showed a protection column that was decreasing, thereby indicating that the ultimate financing is done by the customer. For the record, there was an equity in this plan, but it was very small, so I stuck with my game plan of "equity" or "no-equity" plans and did not even show it. Therefore, for the "FINANCED" plan I showed a cost of $71,697 and no equity.

The second sheet was the one where I showed some plans with cash value. The "DESIGNER" plan was used to appeal to the classy nature of one of the shareholders who conducted his life in very fashionable settings. This plan was a GPL20 on a minimum deposit basis, putting the borrowed funds into single-premium deferred annuities. My purpose here was to enrich the cash value at 30 years by allowing some money for a living buyout, increasing the protection to guard against inflation, and thus presenting a method of competing with Universal Life.

The second plan on the "WITH EQUITY" page was "DEPARTMENT STORE." This was purely and simply a ratebook exposition of GPL20. Both of these last two plans required the same premium, $735,930, but the cash values and protection differed because of the use of the borrowed funds.

The third step in preparation was to construct a sheet showing the two plans together. This was no difficult chore since it only required pasting them together on a large sheet of paper, then using a Xerox machine with a reduction capacity. On the interview, I slowly and carefully explained the "NO-EQUITY" plan, then put it out of sight and reviewed the "WITH EQUITY" plan. Only when I felt that all parties understood the difference in the methods of approaching the creation of funds for the buy-sell agreement did I show the combined sheet. When necessary I covered any sections not under discussion with plain paper so that on the screen only what was pertinent was showing.

The understanding of the proposals was clear to all parties and we focused in on a discussion of the "DESIGNER." The names had silently done their job. We had absolutely no discussion of "Term" or "Permanent"; the words simply did not come up. I had many questions on the reasons why certain schematics created certain differences. Notice that in this illustration, three of the ideas presented are exactly the same plan, GPL20. I had a three-to-one chance of selling ordinary life. There was only one possibility of selling the term. The "BUDGET" plan did not seem appealing, as it shouldn't, for a stock-redemption arrangement. After all, we must consider the very likely contingency that one of the shareholders will wish to retire or sell out during his or her lifetime. Then what good does a noncash-value plan do. My philosophy regarding term plans if the insured lives, is that the premiums were a debt to the insurance company. Both parties fulfilled the terms of the contract: the insured by living and the company by having the fund on standby during the period of coverage. That's great for some situations but not so hot if the insured lives and reflects on the dollars spent but not saved. That is the nature of debt after it is over.

To recap what occurred: I offered four plans for consideration, which is more than I cared to since it does make for a complicated interview. I used the "cut and paste" method of making the proposal, which is actually very easy once I decide which columns I need and I note it on the second sheet of the computer illustrations for the secretary who will be doing the paste-up. The floor usually looks like a movie cutting room after all the slicing and dicing is finished. She then constructs a clean copy by pasting in the ones we want from the original and typing in my goofy names, and then making clear photocopies for the interview. Someday some company will be able to run just the columns I want on one sheet. Then we can get away from ordering out four proposals and then cutting and pasting them into shape. When we're sold these computers, we're told all about the wild and wonderful things they can do. We hear about spreadsheets that can give us 40 columns for ledger statements or only two if that's what we want. I guess that it is possible, but so far I haven't met the operator who can do what I want. I know it's in the machine, but so far we can't make it come out. When it's available, I'll be elated and then I can do some real dreaming about custom-tailored illustrations. I think this idea of showing more than one variation of the same theme on one sheet is fantastic. How many times have you had to go back to your sources and get another run to show a different approach, such as four-pay or disappearing premium, or some other variety? In this particular case, we had to make 12 runs to get down to what you see in illustration 17. We needed three lives times the four approaches, and when it was over, it all came out on one sheet. Even then, we only pasted in cutouts from the computer runs. My goal is to be able to figure in advance what ultimate columns I want and program the machine to spit out a one-page illustration showing it. It will save a lot of time and possibility for errors, considering all the confusing paper that looks exactly alike. We always have to be careful about which stuff we're cutting and which we're pasting back. We check, check, and double-check. I have no doubt that someday, someone else who understands the machine as I do not, will be able to figure out what I want and push a different combination of the same buttons and give me even simpler illustrations.

Illustration 17 is one of the illustrations which did not sell on the first try, so a second interview was needed, which we'll discuss using illustration 18. The reason it did not close is because the clients wanted to talk to another agent and because they had to make a decision about how much premium the business could afford. They assured me they would not show my proposals to the other agent; even if they had, he wouldn't know what I had shown unless he was one of my readers. Even then it would have been unlikely because this was a custom-made blueprint for these clients. I did receive a call back from one of the shareholders, and he told me he was mailing a proposal the other agent had sent outlining Universal Life. He was pleased with me because I had anticipated this and he was prepared for the format of the plan. I studied the Universal Life and called them with my comments, saying the proposal came out just as we had discussed in our original planning session. They said they wished to proceed with me, but they needed various other combinations of amounts. Therefore, on to illustration 18.

Illustration 18 goes with the same case as shown in illustration 17. The titles are not the same because we were now trying to find the right combination of protection and cash value for the proposed buyout. You will observe that I have amounts ranging from $1,000,000 to $500,000. This was in accordance with the desires of the major shareholder, "N." At the bottom of each of the three columns are the initials of the shareholders. In this case, I have not touched them up for anonymity; this is the exact way the sheet was presented for the client. I sometimes do that on illustrations for the sake of space if I think it is too crowded, or for the purpose of having the readers of the reports question themselves just for a moment about what the letters mean. Often, they will ask me before I get to explain all the material what the shorthand-type initials stand for. Then it is something like a Dick Tracy secret-code club. We're talking our own language and doing it efficiently during our business. It also sounds like real big business to be addressed by initials only—something like JFK or LBJ or IBM. In this business there were three of them: N (75 percent shareholder), B (15 percent shareholder), and J (10 percent shareholder). These are the ratios that you will find at the bottom of each amount.

The $800,000 of Increasing Premium is GPL20 for all the shareholders. The $1,000,000 is also GPL20. The third segment is called "Combination Premium"; you will notice the legend that explains this. Next to each initial I have indicated which plan the individual will have. The chief shareholder truly was a brilliant statistics man and he could find the correct mix of plans and amounts from this table that I prepared. He was the one who was interested in having large cash values in the year 2002, which is when he would be 65.

Because of premium restraints, the plan they selected was $500,000 of "Combination Plan." I took the applica-

Illustration 18. Final Fitting

BUSINESS CONTINUATION INSURANCE

Year	$800,000		$1,000,000		$500,000	
	Increasing Premium	Equity	Increasing Premium	Equity	Combination Premium	Equity
1983	$ 8,078	$ 178	$ 10,079	$ 222	$ 5,983	$ 134
1984	8,294	5,340	10,349	6,675	5,946	4,199
1985	8,620	11,226	10,756	14,033	6,048	8,673
1986	8,946	17,834	11,163	22,292	6,152	13,552
1987	9,243	25,165	11,535	31,457	6,237	18,837
1988	9,529	33,212	11,892	41,515	6,317	24,520
1989	9,792	41,979	12,221	52,474	6,384	30,605
1990	10,017	51,453	12,503	64,317	6,430	37,079
1991	10,244	61,653	12,787	77,066	6,479	43,954
1992	10,457	72,574	13,052	90,717	6,519	51,227
1993	10,637	84,218	13,277	105,273	6,541	58,895
1994	10,790	96,581	13,469	120,727	6,548	66,955
1995	10,913	109,662	13,622	137,077	6,541	75,405
1996	10,982	123,450	13,709	154,312	6,499	84,236
1997	11,027	137,937	13,765	172,422	6,447	93,441
1998	11,039	153,127	13,780	191,409	6,374	103,019
1999	11,023	169,006	13,759	211,258	6,285	112,961
2000	10,991	185,590	13,720	231,987	6,190	123,273
2001	10,943	202,877	13,660	253,597	6,085	133,951
2002	10,891	220,879	13,595	276,099	5,980	145,001
2003	10,807	239,607	13,491	299,509	5,861	156,423
2004	8,514	258,252	10,624	322,815	4,449	167,798
2005	7,418	276,752	9,254	345,941	3,804	179,087
2006	6,430	295,062	8,019	368,827	3,207	190,261
2007	5,437	313,118	6,778	391,398	2,605	201,282
2008	4,435	330,891	5,525	413,614	2,000	212,133
2009	3,431	348,366	4,270	435,457	1,390	222,802
2010	2,428	365,560	3,017	456,951	781	233,303
2011	1,523	382,518	1,886	478,148	234	243,662
2012	495	399,286	600	499,108	342 CR	253,909
	$253,374		$316,157		$149,974	

(N- 600)   (N- 750,000)   (N-Inc.- 375)
(B- 120)   (B- 150,000)   (B-Dec.- 75)
(J- 80)   (J- 100,000)   (J-Dec.- 50)

May 10, 1983

tions without going too deeply into the problem of shortfall of coverage since I felt, in my stomach, that enough time had been spent by all of us in coming together on this decision. However, I would have been shortchanging them on service and advice if I did not try to place the $1,000,000 of protection. This was the legitimate amount that was required and the amount that I first heard on the first interview as the value of the business. Too many times, agents allow premium considerations to rob families of the true worth of their shares just because they feel they will jeopardize a sale. I think just the opposite is true and it should be a target goal to do all that is necessary to fund fully. I am not saying a case should be squandered because of overkill, if the clients indicate they are sincere in accepting a lower value later just because of the investment in premiums now. One way of handling it is to agree with the lower amount but order out alternate policies for the full amount. That is what I did in this case. I got the policies they wanted, but I also got additional term policies for the second deck of coverage to the full million.

They took the policies and were happy that they had the right to convert to the "savings type" later on. I didn't even get back into a discussion of the names of the policies because this would have caused another round of "Increasing Premium—No Equity" discussions. It was not necessary. I explained that the health was good enough for the issue of full funding right now. The second layer of contracts are "option" insurance; they give the raw protecton as long as it is desired, then is changed to take care of the sinking-fund concept for the living buyout.

Once again, in preparing this follow-up illustration, I required 12 separate runs from the computer in order to get the sheet that I really needed, that which was a composite for the mix I had selected. For other people the runs as they come fresh from the machine might be the right ones, but for me they are just too much baggage and create more questions and work than is needed or even desired by our customers.

On those occasions when I need a full-blown report because of the circumstances of the case, I absolutely use it. But even then it is not a clean, picture-perfect illustration. I mark it up with direction-finding notes and observations. If it is kept neat and squeaky clean, there is the chance that the client will be over-awed by the dominance of it and not want to make a decision now or even touch it. Of course, this is all a matter of the salesperson's personal preference and whatever works best should be used. My shrunken presentations happen to work well for me, and in the days of low-calorie everything, I think there is merit to this approach in business reports.

*   *   *

7.

LET ME TELL YOU SOMETHING!

When an argument occurs, the phrase, "Let me tell you something" usually gets said. I guess the reason is that one party or the other can hardly wait their turn to spill out the points they think will do the convincing. This is also true of debates, which are not arguments; each person thinks his or her side is the correct one and wants to prepare a place for the words to land. Therefore, the introduction: "Let me tell you something"; or, in other words, "Open your mind, dummy. Here comes something good." Another reason for the introduction before another salvo is courtesy. In order to take part in a two-sided discussion, one has to listen, even if he or she doesn't want to. Then it is assumed that the other faction must also listen. When you feel some real winning serves are about to come out, you grease the skids by letting the other person know that now is the time they should pay attention so that they will realize you are right and they are wrong (or vice versa). It's probably the absolute worst way to do it, but it is done all the time. When the comment is made, can we really believe it is going to make a difference? It will probably make the other party more angry, even if it happens to be right. There is no reasoning in an argument so no one admits to themselves that they are the wrong party, even if the other person has made a valid contention. At that moment, it is customary to change the focus by bringing up the shortcomings of the other contestant; you know, all the little ones that have been saved up for a long time and were going to be overlooked. No good usually comes out of an argument. They take a lot of time to mend afterwards.

Unfortunately, some of us make an argumentative situation out of an interview. A losing tactic in a debate is to have all the cards in your hand, notwithstanding the fact they are the right ones, and not allowing the other party to make any statement at all. The sales process has to be a dialogue, or at least appear to be one. The customer has to choose to be a buyer and not merely be backed into making a move. There must be choices and the opportunity for open and honest exchange. Our proposals or sales presentations are all designed to be winners, but in reality we shouldn't need them at all. The policies themselves should be able to do the selling without any dialogue.

But we know it takes a salesperson to sell our products; they just don't sell all by themselves. There has to be an offer and acceptance before the deal is consummated. In sports, every play, when diagrammed, is pictured as succeeding. Every one of them is drawn to make a score, gain yardage, or make some kind of progress by the effort. In sports there is also a defense side whose job is to thwart the game plan of the offense. There has to be a process of getting the two teams together in one place and having them alternately try their offense and defense against the other offense and defense. The point is that plans on paper don't score unless some person does something to make something happen.

My object with the simplified proposals and interviews is to let the other party make all the points as long as I have instilled the reasoning that leads to those points. Therefore, I use "end" words that I plant in these things that make a statement without all of the diatribe leading up to it. The buyer of products usually has a feel for the real need of them. Our insurance buyers all know they need the products. Our purpose is to make that need imminent and important enough to take it out of the realm of the intangible and post-ponable. Primary to all of our planning is the fact that the benefit is for someone else later on. It is either for benefici-aries or the insured when they are older. I explain that it is not for the person carrying the insurance, but for someone far in-to the future. We don't know who that person is, now. None of us will be the same 40 years from now as we are today.

My real game plan is to get the story out completely and preferably have the buyer side with me, with my saying as few words as possible. People always like their own ideas better. Our clients fully understand that they need our products and, therefore, I try to get them to express that feeling before they assume the posture of an adversary in a sales situation. I will give you a few illustrations where I tried to have the prospect do all the thinking and selling, while I assumed the role of observer and moderator.

When one looks at illustration 19, it doesn't appear to be a selling stimulus at all. It seems to be just a statement of fact. That's what it is; nothing else. I had an interview with a client for whom I had done personal planning but, as yet, had not done the corporate work. The reason was that I had not met one of the other shareholders who was a decision-maker in the corporation; he lived out of state and did not visit Michigan often. Sam was the active employee/shareholder who ran the day-to-day activities here, while Chuck was an investor who originally sponsored all the capital to start the firm.

Initially, they had issued four 25 percent shares in the business in the names of Sam D. and Arlene D., and Chuck J. and Kathy J. Even though there were these four equal

Illustration 19. Do It Yourself Solution

ACME CORPORATION

SAM D. 20%

ARLENE D. 20%

CHUCK J. 20%

KATHY J. 20%

sam d., jr. 20%
(nonvoting)

shareholders, all the decisions were made by Sam and Chuck. In the last year, they had each sold 5 percent of their stock on a reissued basis to Sam, Jr. Now the makeup was four equal 20 percent common-stock owners and one 20 percent non-voting stock owner. This kept the balance equal between Sam and Chuck as far as voting was concerned, but it gave Sam, Jr. a piece of the ownership since he was presently active in the business and would inherit it someday. There was no buy-sell planning. There was a desire for it, but when it was discussed, no one knew how to do it without changing the balance so that the voting stock was still on an equal basis between the two families.

We recently purchased a machine that makes letters of the alphabet in a big, highlighted style, similar to what you see in illustration 19. It has various sizes and styles of type and I think it is a perfect tool for me to use in highlighting some of these abbreviated proposals. You haven't seen any of them yet in the book because we just got access to it and I haven't made any agendas or illustrations with it, save illustration 19. This one proved to be a biggie and we will be capitalizing on the potential of the machine from now on. One thing I can see it doing is names on files for quick and easy reference, but that's for our use. I can see it being used to good effect on agendas, most specifically in putting the person's name on the top. We all like to see ourselves showcased, so putting the name or other things that need stressing in outsize italics or Gothic style will add some appeal to our proposals. The name will grab attention; no one takes lightly a piece of paper that features him or her in such prominence.

For Chuck, the business was an investment, but not his primary one. Kathy, his wife, was his sole beneficiary, and his only concern was for her to derive a good deal of profit out of it after his death. Sam had no objection to this from the point of taking care of Kathy, but for the ultimate planning he wanted Sam, Jr. to become involved on a true voting basis. A stock-redemption would change the mix of ownership among the voting people. Whenever I spoke of it, the feelings became heated because no one really wanted to make a decision now to invest in premiums and the problem didn't seem too big today since everything was going well and all sides were happy with the results. So why even think of a real future problem.

Let me shorten the planning lesson by saying that the solution would really be simple if we could get all the parties to agree on the consequences after a death. The solution lay in having more than one type of buyout agreement. For certain owners it would be stock redemption and for others it would be cross purchase. But the direct purpose of this illustration was to get Sam, Jr., who along with his father were the real operators of the business, involved on a voting basis. I did what I always do for myself when I have a knotty problem of stock ownership; I sat down with the clean backside of a computer illustration, which I use as scrap paper. (This now answers the question of what I do with all the waste after simmering down all the paper onto one page. I don't throw it away. There's too much of it.)

I drew squares representing the individual shareholders and a big one representing Acme Corporation. I put "sam d., jr. 20% nonvoting" in small letters and drew a line above his name; this reminded me of the difference in his stock flavor from the others. I then made more assumptions as to what would happen to the percentages if various individuals were the first to die. After a while I have lines and arrows and lettering going in all directions, but the solution comes out. I actually do this tick-tack-toe-type doodling in many cases. It is easier to spot solutions when you can see the entities and relationships, spread out on a sheet in front of you. You can use erasers or scissors or other means to change the graphics until you come up with the correct picture.

It became clear to me that I could make a decent suggestion for the orderly and economical transfer of the ownership interests at death. I had one drawing outlining this: if Sam dies, Sam, Jr. buys his stock on a cross-purchase basis. This does nothing to change the mix since Sam, Jr. still only owns 20 percent of the voting rights; he can't vote his 20 percent nonvoting stock. Sam, Jr. could have the same deal with his mother. If Sam, Jr. dies, his stock could revert on a stock-redemption deal or even pass on to the other children.

Chuck could make a stock-redemption agreement with Acme so that Kathy would have cash and not paper at his death, while the other family would have the business. I also outlined that if Chuck were the first to die, the stock-redemption death agreement for him would also trigger a life buyout for Kathy's stock. There were all kinds of possibilities for accomplishing what was desired.

I had about three solutions when I decided it was goofy for me to make a final suggestion for something that I felt would appear obvious if the shareholders did exactly the same thing I was now doing on my format papers. That's when I made illustration 19. I took one of the blank drawings I had made and had a secretary use the lettering machine to make illustration 19 for me. Then I called Sam and said I had a solution for the problem that was plaguing him. I decided I would let him doodle the same as I was and maybe he had a better suggestion. I took one of the typed illustrations as opposed to my handwritten ones, and lettered in the solution you see above regarding the cross-purchase and stock redemptions. We went to lunch and I talked about the problem again until I could see Sam was uneasy. Then I took out the drawing I had made and explained it. I said it surely was not the final one but something along those lines would solve the problem. I gave him a blank one and let him start filling in the lines. This became a do-it-yourself sale. He did it. He really became enthusiastic. He made slight revisions and thought about other possibilities for other, younger children who may be involved in the business later on. But from the time I gave him the crosswordlike paper and he took out his pen, I did very little except look on and say, "Hmmm."

He contacted Chuck in the other city and became the sponsor of the idea instead of me. We had the usual paperwork and lawyer involvement and a large sale resulted.

I think the point here is that we do not have ιo have all the answers. They may look too contrived and patterned. Let the client get involved as much as possible. He or she is really interested in the proper solution and it means much more if they can derive a sense of authorship. Maybe the old excuse, "I don't want to get involved," has a place in selling—that is, if we can shift the right ideas to the other parties.

Complex situations can be made very attractive when they are simplified. But I must caution that sincerity is a big part of this. We have to be sincere and at the same time indicate our own confidence; otherwise, our simplifying can communicate to the listener that we think he or she isn't too bright. There can be more than one meaning to the same phrase.

As an example, think of the times you have gotten directions in a strange neighborhood. I know I have had different reactions to the phrase "You can't miss it." Depending on how it is said, I immediately know whether it is easy to get to this place or not. I better listen carefully because it sounds like my direction-giver is really saying that he's convinced HE can't miss it from here. What comes across quickly is that he or she either is or is not a good teacher. Frankly, on occasion, I have been scared to death that I will miss the destination, just from the way that someone says, "You can't miss it from here." One has to be a highly qualified communicator to use simplified methods, and one also has to be a highly qualified communicator to use technical methods. In the final analysis the difference between the two may be razor-thin. For different agents, different methods will work at different times. I find that the simple method is the safer one for me.

The thought crosses my mind that "simple" can sometimes be an insult or even a challenge. I approach all toys that advertise that they are "so simple that a six-year-old can put it together," with the greatest suspicion or fear. If possible, I even avoid them. I always wonder if it's a test of the mentality of the one who is doing the assembling. Usually, the instructions and pictures are scanty. Then there are the other traps that are built in, such as instructions for a "TA4C" unit, while the one you have is a "TA4CP." Another trap comes in the form of an extra screw or a missing one. I have had units to put together where the hardware is for the wrong unit.

These examples of erroneous information or missing parts should be a lesson to us that there is no shortcut to a proper presentation. Using a simplified presentation requires an exercise of judgment, depending on the users. Some agents use just a yellow pad of paper or nothing at all, and it works very effectively. Others feel that the computer can do all the necessary work by pumping out all the displays one would want to see. I'm sure all of you have used all the methods just mentioned, and various combinations of each. So have I and I guess the watchword is "whatever suits." Each interview is a new encounter and must be approached differently, just as a meal in a restaurant will taste completely different on two different days. Sometimes, it may need more condiments or seasoning than at other times. The same reasoning holds true with each new interview. My intention with the tailored presentations and agendas are the main courses, which is the need. The rest are the appetizers.

The object of illustration 20 is to try to allow the client to see the strong points before he or she makes a commitment and then has to substantiate a position. I want that stance to be a positive one from the start. Therefore, I try to make a nonverbal statement before I make one verbally. What I mean is that I want the prospect to spot some meaning in these illustrations so that he or she is yearning to hear more about the plan. Open-mindedness is the result of an inquisitive nature. When the mind is open, we stand a chance of reaching a fair decision.

Illustration 20. Blueprint for Savings

WILL SMITH
CAM-FOR DISTRIBUTORS, INC.
$200,000 COVERAGE

Policy Year	(K-Mart) Increasing Premium	(Pierre Cardin) Increasing Premium
1	$ 646	$ 929
2	708	961
3	772	1,249
4	844	1,567
5	922	1,899
6	1,008	2,229
7	1,116	2,543
8	1,238	2,857
9	1,386	3,163
10	1,566	3,457
11	1,776	3,747
12	2,012	4,027
13	2,246	4,291
14	2,512	4,537
15	2,814	4,779
16	2,538	5,003
17	2,720	4,769
18	2,890	4,545
19	2,776	4,317
20	3,080	4,087

Total Premiums	$35,570	$61,080
Total Equity	— 0 —	$56,040 (Tax Free)
Total Free Continuing Insurance	— 0 —	93,800 (Tax Free)
	(CML YRT 100)	(CML 15 GPL)

January 1983

This illustration for the substituted name of Will Smith, is not too unlike others you have seen already. The client needed $200,000 of key-man insurance for corporate use. The business was custom home-building, so Will was fully familiar with the quality of the lower-priced products. He asked me for a term quote and I said I would have one drawn up. When we met again in my office, I had already run the proposals from the computer and done the cut-and-paste routine for two plans: term to 100, and 15-Year Graded Premium Life. You are now familiar with my two-column comparisons. My object here was to place the equity product as opposed to the term.

The difference in premiums is not great, but by year 16 the ordinary is coming down in premiums by use of dividends, while the term is still on the climb. There were two significant things in this illustration that helped make the sale. One of them will be easily spotted when you look at the illustration. The other cannot be spotted because the book does not contain color pictures. What you will notice immediately are the titles I put over the plans. Both of them were increasing premium, even though the GPL 15 had an equity, which I mentioned in the summary lines at the bottom. Since this company was a custom home-builder and prided itself on its name, I decided to use labels that indicated higher quality versus lower price. I called the one plan "K-Mart" and the other "Pierre Cardin." He noticed the names immediately and all of his questions keyed in on the GPL 15. In fact, he had none about the term even though that's what he had asked me to quote.

You might be thinking this proposal should have been in a section of the book dealing with titles and you would be right, except for something you can't see from this illustration as reproduced here. Remember this section is about simplifying the complex. The illustration as you see it seems to be working very well and it does a good job of selling the steak and not the sizzle. The difference here is that I had the illustration made on blueprint paper. Since the client is in the construction business and is used to looking at blueprints all the time, I thought this would be a good time to talk to the client on his or her own terms. I took out the blueprint and gave it to him and he never said a word about the paper it was on. He didn't skip a beat and we went right to work; he was so much in his own element that he felt comfortable.

I have used this approach before when dealing with people who work with blueprints and it has always worked well. I have even done agendas on blueprint paper. We have the prints made at a copy shop that does this kind of work for engineers and construction people. I think it's a bother when we take our little one or two pages into a shop that makes copies of prints up to many feet long and wide for massive projects. They charge us a couple of bucks, which makes it a lot more expensive than the office copy, but it is infinitely more effective.

For clarity's sake I mention that the symbols at the bottom of the columns represent Connecticut Mutual Yearly Renewable Term to 100 (CML YRT 100), and Connecticut Mutual 15-Year Graded Premium Life (CML 15 GPL). I find I must have a code for myself and staff regarding what the plans are that we show. Sometimes I fool my own staff with the offbeat names I put on plans, so we have started putting symbols at the bottom of the plans. It proves to be helpful when we make more than one proposal for the same client. Sometimes we have confusion when they all start looking alike and the only differences are minor. However, I promise you the confusion is nothing like the mishmash that occurs when we store five or six full computer runs for the same case. (Incidentally, I have permission to use the names of Connecticut Mutual's plans; I have been disguising other companies' plan names that showed up on the original untouched versions. Other than the covering or changing of names, nothing else has been changed on these illustrations.)

I have shown you a lot of the ideas I use for dressing up our offerings to clients. Some may think we have a great deal of money tied up in equipment. We really don't. We happen to have our own personal computer, which is tied into the home office by phone modem. We have the usual assortment of typewriters and other office equipment, but beyond that we use simple inexpensive implements. I don't think putting out two dollars to do a proposal on blueprints is too exorbitant if it almost guarantees a sale. There is not too much expense in colored pencils or rubber stamps. Our real forte is being just the slightest bit inventive and catching the client's fancy. If you can't afford some of these devices, don't go into hock; join forces with other agents and share the cost. But there is an old adage about spending money to make money. It's true. But we can't blow too much dough at the office-supply or art-supply store just ordering some cardboard or small tools of someone else's trade. Please accept the fact that the days of the home offices supplying everything are gone. They should not have to. If a person is not willing to invest large or even small amounts of money in his or her business, why should someone else do it?

The illustration we just examined (illustration 20) was rather simple in that it contained only two plans and, therefore, only two columns of numbers. In this case, the object was to show more than one plan to a man who was an owner of an engineering shop and was a very astute professional who prided himself on understanding all the aspects of a situation before he acted. When I met him, he already had quotes and specimen policies from more than one company for this million-dollar intended purchase. I felt I did not want to get too deeply involved with showing every paragraph of a policy and then running back for more "inspections." This was a good test for my type of proposals. I thought to myself that this will tell me if they are really any good for a person who by training is schooled in finding stress points and durability, and who questions everything from first renderings through final inspection.

I decided to show what was asked for—"the best term policy on the market." I knew that the client meant the

Illustration 21. Slide Rule Expert's Blueprint

$1,000,000

Year	A Age 48	B Nonsmoker	Preferred Age 49	C Life	Age 48	Connecticut Mutual (Yearly Renewable)
1	$ 2,660	$ 1,855		$ 2,330		$ 3,780
2	3,490	2,905		3,030		4,140
3	4,790	4,025		3,830		4,550
4	6,520	5,285		4,800		4,970
5	8,220	6,505		5,820		5,450
	$ 25,680		$ 20,575		$ 19,810	$22,890
6	11,070	8,135		6,890		6,030
7	13,580	9,825		7,980		6,850
8	15,440	12,845		9,200		7,820
9	18,270	15,785		10,560		8,910
10	21,630	18,665		11,950		9,990
	79,990		65,255		46,580	39,600
11	25,620	22,755		14,780		11,220
12	30,390	22,815		18,050		12,620
13	33,120	26,615		16,270		11,120
14	39,670	30,405		19,830		11,900
15	47,530	34,205		23,910		12,600
	176,330		136,795		92,840	59,460
16	55,750	38,005		28,120		13,060
17	55,320	41,805		32,840		13,640
18	54,900	45,595		38,090		14,680
19	*20th yr. cash value-$250,000	49,395		43,940		16,340
20	*15th yr. cash value-$228,000	53,195	227,995	50,310	193,300	18,120
	$275,770					75,840

cheapest policy in the near period and not the enduring best. But I took his words to heart and had our receptionist prepare illustration 21. I gave her the format for what I wanted to show. It would once again be the strung-out columns. I was going to use only three plans and put the one I wanted to sell in the center, but Tracey came to me and said she had just received a new rate card in the mail that day and the rates were "lowly" touted. I told her to put in another plan and put the CML on the outside last column. We used names of companies since the client had asked us to research one of them.

I had the illustration done on the same blueprint format we discussed in illustration 20 and the interview went very smoothly. The typewritten figures are the ones that we prepared originally. The handwritten figures outside the five-year periods are cumulative totals for the last five-year span. This is the only change we were requested to calculate. I'm kind of glad we were asked to calculate the comparative figure this way because it certainly answered his questions in favor of the policy I felt, and he discovered, was in his best interest. Significantly, the proposal did its work. It sufficiently answered the queries of a person whose abilities for digging for the baseline foundations I respect.

The goal of all of these one-pagers is to make a sale. But putting it another way, by highlighting the important stuff, I try to get the customer to buy rather than get sold, and I want him to place an order with me for what I feel is the best product for the circumstances. It's a reverse psychology kind of selling, but it works better when the buyer becomes the salesperson and the seller becomes an agent in the truest sense of the word.

Here are the specs in this case (illustration 22). The first plan on the left was sold in 1980. It was for $200,000 on a 62-year-old corporate president. I was a part of the planning team with the attorney and C.P.A. There was considerable other insurance and legal planning, but this policy was de-

Illustration 22. Getting Your Money's Worth

SECTION 303 INSURANCE

Year	ORIGINAL ISSUE $200,000		STANDARD ISSUE $251,824		STANDARD ISSUE $200,000	
	Net Premium	Cash Value	Net Premium	Cash Value	Net Premium	Cash Value
1980	$ 14,347	$ 312	$ 14,347	$ 312	$ 11,397	$ 312
1981	13,365	6,822	13,365	6,822	10,415	6,822
1982	12,743	13,310	12,743	13,396	9,793	13,310
1983	12,187	19,760	11,836	21,584	9,237	19,760
1984	11,679	26,154	11,140	29,706	8,729	26,154
1985	11,167	32,466	10,461	37,730	8,217	32,466
1986	10,687	38,674	9,817	45,628	7,737	38,674
1987	10,223	44,764	9,199	53,381	7,273	44,764
1988	9,779	50,734	8,611	60,982	6,829	50,734
1989	9,351	56,594	8,046	68,441	6,401	56,594
1990	8,979	62,364	7,542	75,780	6,029	62,364
1991	8,621	68,072	7,069	83,034	5,671	68,072
1992	8,277	73,732	6,615	90,220	5,327	73,730
1993	7,939	79,336	6,173	97,342	4,989	73,336
1994	7,613	84,874	5,649	104,382	4,663	84,874
1995	7,323	90,306	5,272	111,296	4,373	90,306
1996	7,047	95,592	4,912	118,037	4,097	95,592
1997	6,775	100,700	4,560	124,561	3,825	100,700
1998	6,511	105,614	4,218	130,843	3,561	105,614
1999	6,257	110,328	3,888	136,873	3,307	110,328
20-Year Totals:	$190,470	$110,328	$165,464	$136,873	$131,470	$110,328
20-Year Net Cost:	*** $80,142 ***		*** $28,591 ***		*** $21,142 ***	
20-Year Avg. Ins:	*** $200,000 ***		*** $251,824 ***		*** $200,000 ***	

August 16, 1982

signed for section 303 estate-tax redemption purposes. The client had a health situation that required an extra premium, making the total $14,347 in column 1, instead of $11,397 in column 5.

At the lower right you will see the date of this revision is August 16, 1982. We had had him reexamined and his health had improved to the point where he was standard. Because of this change, there was a small refund and the future premiums were decreased by about $3,000, as shown by the difference between column 1 and column 5. It was 1982, and the company was in an auto-related business. My goal was to have the company continue to pay the same premium and get a greater cash and protection benefit. The other choice would be to take the lower premium, which would most likely be a welcome thing in the current Detroit economy, and I could very easily see the corporation's viewpoint if that was their choice.

It was the kind of thing where I could sense the decision would be a quick "yes" or a quick "no." All the medical and underwriting work had already been done and it was a new case if I could get agreement. There was a need for the protection, but I knew full well there was also a dire need for cash-flow in the business. My project was to design a proposal that would sell itself. In part one, which is the first set of columns, I showed the existing plan with extra premium. In the third set of columns I showed the result without the extra. If you compare, you will see that the cash value is precisely the same, but the premium reflects the reduction.

The center section represents a money-purchase philosophy of merging section three with a new policy purchased by the former extra, which can now be used as productive premium instead of pure loading. We ran the proposal for the new premium and it increased the face amount by $51,824. Therefore, this center section, although it is displayed here as only two columns of premium and values, is really a policy of $200,000 and one of $51,824 combined. Frankly, the cash

values on any one of the policies did not mean very much in
this plan since the purpose was strictly death redemption.
However, the values were important to the corporate net
worth and made a big difference to the financial statements.
Because of this, I felt it was important to show the line at the
bottom called, "20-YEAR NET COST." I also felt it was important to restate the higher insurance amount, so I put that
at the bottom ("20-YEAR AVG. INS") as well as at the top
under the names of the plans.

I called the plans "ORIGINAL ISSUE," "STANDARD
ISSUE," and "STANDARD ISSUE," the difference between center and right being the face amounts "$251,824,"
and "$200,000," respectively.

The one really unique thing about this proposal was the
color-coding of the three plans. The left section was plain
typewriting, the center was covered with green acetate (box-
ed, in text, for clarity), the right was covered with red acetate
(tinted grey in text). Once again, the proposal was classy in
appearance, but designed to lead to a conclusion. The acetate
can be purchased at an office supply for about 25¢ per sheet.
We used appromixately one-tenth of a sheet in making this
outline, so we did not have a lot of money invested in it. But
the result could be a lot of money to the corporation and a
nice commission to the agent.

The owner called in the company comptroller who was a
man I had worked with before and who I could not read too
well in advance. He was completely objective and very pro-
tective of the company both from the insurance viewpoint
and from a current-cash viewpoint. So, I did not know what
impact his observations would have. Although there was no
question about who made the decisions in this company, the
president carefully and respectfully heeded the advice of his
comptroller, who was a good man. In my mind I felt the decision would be made equally from the input of both men.
They were happy that the extra money could be removed.

They were joyful for the fact that the president's health had improved, as well as for the fact that the improvement would be reflected monetarily for the company. There were many questions, but the key ones had to do with how the center section could have a larger equity after 20 years than their present policy, while at the same time requiring less total premiums than the present policy. I explained that in the center columns the premiums were compounded, which resulted in both higher cash value and dividend earning capacity, as compared to their present policy which did not. The comptroller was especially enthralled with the fact that in the 20th year, the premiums for the center and right plans were similar, yet the cash value was $26,000 greater.

When the talking was done and the moment of silence indicated the moment of decision, the president looked at the comptroller and said, "What do you think, Art?" He responded, "The corporation would be better off with the center section, but the decision is yours."

Then, I received what I felt was my finest compliment, honoring my efforts at effective communications through illustrations. The president said, "We'll take the green."

*　　*　　*

8.

NITPICKING

I spoke about a word making a difference. I have shown colors and lines and abbreviations that lead to a conclusion. It's the small things that make the difference. Sometimes a single line on a piece of paper makes you an airline passenger or leaves you on the ground. When I fly I usually try to have my travel agent get me seat assignments at the same time the tickets are ordered. This lets me choose the seat I want with the certainty of getting it and also saves check-in time at the airport. When I arrive I can just get on the plane without standing in line.

On one recent flight, I followed my usual pattern and waited until it was almost flight time and walked on the plane. The stewardess told me that I would have to go back to the ticket counter and check in. I told her that was already done and I had a boarding pass with a seat number already. She said she saw that but told me, "You have to get slashed." I surely did not understand what she meant so I asked. She explained that all tickets had to have a green slash across a certain part of them. I asked what that had to do with sitting down in this reserved seat. She said it had nothing to do with the seat and I did have mine reserved but she needed the slash.

I assured her I was not attempting to be obstinate but I was not going out to get someone to put a green slash on my ticket when it had nothing to do with my sitting down. She in- sisted I return and get slashed and I refused. I told her she could take the ticket, have it slashed, and return it to me in seat 6B. Just then the ticket agent happened to come on board and she told him her predicament, which apparently was major to her. He said he would take the ticket out and do whatever had to be done.

The whole incident amounts to a pile of nothing, but it illustrates the power of systems. To this young lady, it was vital that all the paperwork was right before the plane took off. I feel much the same way regarding all the paperwork but to my mind that means a low-cal menu. This brings me to the subject of what today's businessman is familiar with seeing as his paperwork. A few years ago, I read a Sunday supplement article concerning the reasons why businesses fail. I jumped to what I thought was an obvious conclusion: underfunding or lack of capital. This was the second most prevalent reason. First was lack of records. When I got into the article, I real- ized that it was absolutely true. Too many businesses pay all their attention to outside activities and lose the ballgame because there is no backup in the office. This gave me an idea for doing agendas or proposals for some of the common in- terviews we do for business situations. I determined that the successful businesspeople I dealt with were all inundated by computer reports, either their own or ones from their suppli- ers. I also observed that they liked clear, concise reports that came in memo form. I came to realize they were good not on- ly because they had a goal but also because, in an instant, they knew the results of days, weeks, months, or years to date. They liked comparisons of all kinds. They could predict trends for the near future or the long haul. They were adept at reading comparative reports. I then decided I would attempt to do my documentation for them in report form whenever I could.

I adopted the agenda format for conducting interviews, which I started calling "meetings" instead of "interviews." You have seen a number of these and you know the philosophy behind their use. I also developed some standard meeting prototypes for the kinds of situations we face over and over again. In this chapter, I will show you three of them that have worked remarkably well for me and endure with little or no change, meeting after meeting after meeting.

I saw the businessowner's ability to grasp things quickly from a report that showed alternatives. The owner worked daily in an atmosphere of choices, the two primary ones being wholesale and retail. No matter where you go in this land, when you are around businessowners, you will hear these words regularly. These are the mainstays of staying in business; you buy for one price and you sell for another, obviously one should be better than the other and if you are successful at doing it right, another word is heard: profits. When you as a vendor of products to the businessperson mention these words, you get attention. I developed illustration 23 for the purpose of giving attention to the problems of transferring a business interest at death. I gathered all the thoughts I could about the reasons for and against each method and it seemed to me a "wholesale" approach to the transfer made more sense and resulted in more profit.

The title of the report is, "Methods of Transferring Business Interest at Death." It was designed to take advantage of quick eye-shifting from left to right and comparison of the one method to the other. As I mentioned, businesspeople are adept at making comparisons. The two comparisons I have them make are "A-Retail" and "B-Wholesale." Obviously, they are conditioned to like the wholesale idea better than retail. I tried to put into this proposal all the objections I had ever heard regarding buying business buyout insurance. I

Illustration 23. Wholesale-Retail

METHODS OF TRANSFERRING BUSINESS INTEREST AT DEATH

	A-RETAIL	B-WHOLESALE
Date of Payment:	After death.	Before death.
Principal Payments on Stock:	Yes	No
Interest Payments:	Yes	Yes
Amount of Principal:	Determined after death—subject to negotiations with heirs, survivors, attorneys, IRS, and other advisors.	Set in advance by agreement.
Amount of Interest:	Variable—determined after death—assume very favorable rate—8%.	3.2%
Actual Cost:	Full value of shares plus interest = 100% plus interest.	Full value of interest payments paid by date of death. No principal payments. Never reaches 100%.
Timing of Payments:	Start at date of death.	Start discounted payments now. Stop at date of death.
Payments Carried on Books:	Yes—liability after death for negotiated value of shares.	Yes—as asset before death for exact stated equity value of interest payments.
Stock Encumbered After Death:	Yes	No
Buyer at Death:	Unknown—not specified	Set in advance by agreement.
Estate Obligated to Sell at Death:	No	Yes
Discounted Value of Principal and Interest Available at Date of Death, in One Sum:	No	Yes
Payments Waived at Disability of Shareholder:	No	Yes
"Pegged Value" for Estate Taxes:	No	Yes

A. Installment payments after death either to heirs or bank, cash if available, reserve account, borrow on any buy-now-pay-later plan.

B. Life insurance.

listed these on the left-hand side as items for consideration. Then I made the comparisons in the next two columns.

Line 1, "Date of Payment," clearly shows the distinction between having the funding or not having it. This is the basic point I have to make and I try to say it out loud as early in the interview as possible: "Somebody has to pay something, someday." This point alone does not make a great deal of difference since it does entail paying something.

Line 2, "Principal Payments on Stock," depicts a rather substantial difference between the methods: not having to pay for the stock under the "wholesale" method. I often get the question at this point, "How can that be done?" I always answer it with one of my favorites, "I don't know, but I will get you a contract that will prove it."

Line 3, "Interest Payments," regards interest and I indicate there is interest to pay in either place. The question of deductibility does not always come up, but when it does, I answer it as follows: "The interest is deductible under the 'retail' but not under the 'wholesale.' " There is a good, solid financial reason for that. Interest is deductible because it is a wasting cost and not an asset. The interest under the "wholesale" method is a special kind of interest that is not even spent. I'll come to the reason in a moment.

Line 4, "Amounts of Principal," deals with the amount that has to be paid. In this line under "retail," I put in all the variations and uncertainties of an unwritten and unfunded arrangement. I speak of situations of relatives, second husbands or wives, attorneys, or others giving cheap and harmful advice at some later date. Among these other advisors I once had the situation of a young widow holding up a buyout where the insurance was issued but the agreement, although drawn, was never signed. The negotiations, which should have never existed in the first place, dragged out for months and the ultimate price was almost double the amount that had been agreed upon and insured. When they finally settled, the surviving shareholder asked the widow who was advising her and why she was so determined. She replied that since the buyout had not yet been paid and she was not getting the salary of her late husband, she had to take a job. She had a 62-year-old friend of the family who was the babysitter who told her, "I'm a widow too, honey. Don't let them cheat you. Keep asking for more." Actually, the excess payout will take 15 years to complete and is causing a great strain on the business. The fault of not having the contract signed lay with one of the shareholders who kept questioning the terms and never made a priority effort to read and complete what the other shareholders had started.

Line 5, "Amount of Interest," shows very vividly the difference between the interest rates of the two methods. Sometimes the discussion will bring out the fact that the partners would agree to "No" interest. Please do your homework now and look up the IRS regulations on "imputed" interest. There are varying rates for the length of the buyout and for the year in which it was executed. This is enforced even if there is a signed agreement in force. If this point arises, it is an excellent place to show your knowledge and further enhance the dire need for a "wholesale" plan.

In Line 5 in the "wholesale" column, I have put "3.2%." This is the premium stated as a percentage. In this case, it happened to be a composite premium for three lives. The average of the three was $32 per thousand, so I expressed it as "3.2%." This is also an aid to place rated cases. If the rate should come back at $40 per thousand, I would start the interview by saying, "I have good news; I have coverage for everyone. If you will recall, the price I quoted was 3.2 percent, which was prime rate. I still have a good rate at 4 percent." It works pretty well and I don't have to blame anyone's health, the underwriting, or anything else.

I also use this line to get ready for any extra premium. Suppose I suspect there is going to be a rating. I will then build in some cushion on the original illustration. I might put in 5 percent. If the policies come back at a lower premium, I then say, "The rate that I showed you was a good rate, but after medical underwriting, I have a better one; in fact, it is almost prime at 4 percent."

No matter what the rate, it is still less than any interest that will be assessed after death, either by the bank or under the IRS imputed rate, which starts at a low of 7 percent. I often never have to quote any figures other than this percentage. Sometimes we have to get into insurance plans and detailed figures and that's where I use some of the other illustrations you have already seen. But most often, we only use illustration 23.

Line 6, "Actual Cost," for "retail" shows that in no instance will less than 100 percent of the value required for the buyout be paid. With interest, it will come to more than the full value of the stock or partnership interest. Under "wholesale," I explain that the interest payments that have been made are special in that they are sufficient to discount anything else that would otherwise be due if this method were not used. This is another reason that this kind of interest is not deductible. You as the agent will recognize this line as the premium.

Line 7, "Timing of Payments," is a repeat of Line 1. I have found that this part of the interview really grabs the attention of the parties and I want to restate our basic insurance function of paying for it in advance of the death. It is also necessary to remind the listeners that something has to be paid by somebody, someday.

Line 8, "Payments Carried on the Books," shows the effect of either insuring or not insuring. Without a funded buyout, the ultimate price paid has to be shown somewhere. In this country, we keep score with books. If a "retail" buyout occurs and there is one million dollars owed to someone, it has to be booked. It is there for suppliers, Dun and Bradstreet, banks, and anyone else who needs access to the company financial papers to see. If the money is owed, it has to be paid sometime and having it as a liability sure does not make for smooth-and-easy operation.

In the same line, under "wholesale," I show the cash values. They also have to be booked if they are corporate assets. This forestalls the objection of "spending our money" since the reasoning of a transfer of capital applies here. Also, this is the place where I restate the case for the nondeductibility of the "interest" payments. They are not deductible because they are not spent. They are still in the corporation for use if necessary, or if not, they are an asset adding strength to the balance sheet.

Line 9, "Stock Encumbered After Death," is strictly a selling point showing the hazard of doing nothing. If a buyout is arranged after death, the stock is pledged to it and cannot be dealt with for other progressive purposes later on. If a merger or acquisition were available, the problem of a superior lien against the stock is present. Free dealing is restricted and prospective investors may not like coming into a business that is mortgaged to a deceased shareholder's heirs. Under "wholesale," this is obviated.

Line 10, "Buyer at Death," concerns the fact that nothing is for sure under "retail." It's all in the hands of the gods, chance, luck, or charity. With a "wholesale" arrangement, it is predetermined who will own the business. Without preplanning, it is not certain who will own the business. It could be a surprise who comes out of the pile when there is a random scuffle by the heirs to get the best possible deal out of a bad situation.

Line 11, "Estate Obligated To Sell at Death," often brings up some lively conversation among the owners. Sometimes, families will have enough outside income or means of support so that the sale of the business is not necessary. They may feel it is a good idea to hang onto the business just as an investment. It may be a better idea if the interest inherited is a majority position. Then there is the chance for determining dividend policy so that income or other compensation will flow. This, of course, has the opposite effect for the minority faction. With a "wholesale" agreement in effect, it is known who presently owns the business, who should own it and, most importantly, who *will* own it.

Line 12, "Discounted Value of Principal and Interest," deals with the payment of ALL money that is required to finalize the transaction. This includes principal and interest. It ain't there under "retail." It is under "wholesale."

Line 13, "Payments Waived at Disability of Shareholder," always brings a lot of discussion. The beauty of all these points is that clients see both sides before I have to say anything. This way, if there are varying opinions among the principals, it comes out. The queries sometimes take the form of wonderment as to what the other partner would really do if he or she were the survivor, or what that person would do if the other partner died first. The discussions about disability really get entangled. When I say that I can waive payments on everything if a disability happens, I again get asked, "How can you do that?" I answer, "I don't know, but I will give you a contract that proves it." It leads to further discussions about the merits of disability buyout insurance.

Line 14, " 'Pegged Value' for Estate Taxes," is self-explanatory to the trained life insurance person, but it is often a revelation to the owners that the taxing authorities will apply the doctrine of the "open till" to the final numbers on the worth of the business. They are incredulous when I tell them that the three or four methods used by the IRS can vary between double and triple each other. It also rankles them that the estate will have to pay for the evaluations that give the ammunition to the IRS to start calculations regarding what is owed.

When I have finished making this presentation, I read the legend at the bottom, "A. Installment payments after death either to heirs or bank, cash if available, reserve account, or any buy-now-pay-later plan...B. Life insurance."

We have this presentation stored in our word processor. There are only a few variables on the sheet so I can be ready for an interview in about two minutes. I just have to tell my secretary that I want a "retail-wholesale at 2.6% for a partnership." She will then change the words "stock" and "corporation" for "partner" and "partnership."

Deferred compensation is a complicated technical subject. If you have not yet studied it, I suggest you start your work on a quiet Saturday when the interruptions are minimal. Illustration 24 is not meant to be the finale to your education. On the contrary, it is only a beginning to a sale if you have the background knowledge to answer the questions that will come when you broach the subject with your prospects. In many instances, it is the finale to the presentation and no other material is needed. This is frequently the case. I present this one that I have named, "An Exchange of Promises," and there is no need for other submissions. This comes from a pretty good knowledge of the tax laws that govern the program and the fact that this confidence shows through when doing an interview. Frankly, unless the client wants to know more of the circuitry of a deferred compensation agreement with proper funding, he can rest assured about his program knowing nothing other than what is on this one page.

Deferred compensation can be called "Salary Continuance" or some other names that have to do with delaying compensation until a later date. Pension and profit-sharing plans are deferred compensation, as are IRA plans. The ones just mentioned are what is known as "qualified," which means they fall into a prescribed legal framework providing like benefits for employees in like situations. In this regard they are deductible plans, which means the employer can deduct them from the taxable income of the company even though the employee is not currently taxed on the amounts saved. The item we will speak of in this illustration is not a

Illustration 24. Exchange of Promises

SELECTIVE SALARY CONTINUANCE
(AN EXCHANGE OF PROMISES)

CORPORATION PROMISES: **IF**   **EXECUTIVE PROMISES:**

1. To continue $25,000 salary for 10 years after retirement.

2. If executive should die before retirement, continue $25,000 salary to family for 10 years.

3. Corporation will set aside $455 per month in sinking fund.

1. To remain with corporation until age 65.

2. Not to compete with corporation after retirement.

3. Be available for consultation after retirement.

RIGHTS OF PARTIES

CORPORATION: **EXECUTIVE:**

1. Right to use sinking fund for any other proper corporate use. This includes borrowing, investing, pledging, etc.

2. Corporation reserves right to limit total cost of promise to $5,243.

1. No change from present.

OBLIGATION OF PARTIES

CORPORATION: **EXECUTIVE:**

1. Place $455 per month with fiduciary.

1. No change from present.

deductible item; therefore, it does not have to qualify equally for all employees. The true name for this concept should be "Nonqualified Deferred Compensation."

In this particular illustration I used the term "Selective Salary Continuance." Then I gave it a subtitle, "An Exchange of Promises." This really sets the tone for the interview and lets the parties know that there are tradeoffs between the company and the executive. It is a phrase that is not very hard to understand. Both parties are ready for the fact of conditions being set. I then break the page up into two columns. On the one side I list the corporation and on the other, the executive. The first section has to do with the benefits that are being promised and the conditions that have to be met in order to have them. The corporation promises to continue a salary of $25,000 for 10 years after retirement. I don't bother getting into the ages or dates of retirement. These are details that can be worked out when it comes time to draw up the legal papers. In this particular case, it was intended to have a normal retirement date of age 65.

The corporation also promises to continue a salary of $25,000 for 10 years to the beneficiary of the executive if he should die before retirement. These amounts will be paid in addition to any retirement, government, or other payments the executive may have. These benefits are purely arbitrary and are set differently for each case, depending on what the circumstances of the individual and corporation are. They could be stated as flat amounts, as I have done here, or they can be a stated percentage of compensation, such as 25% or 50%.

The next item is one that does not even have to be stated in the formal documents the corporation will draw up for this deal. It is implied that the corporation will pay the benefits as they are due and that there is no need for advance funding. It would make no sense at all for a small- or medium-sized corporation to promise these things and not have a way to pay them if the contract should come due immediately because of an early death. It could break a company to have to pay these amounts if it loses an employee who formerly helped produce revenue. The same is true for the benefits at retirement. Direct pay can be a heavy burden if the money has not been prefunded and allowed to earn interest to help assist the stipend. If you want to get a clear picture of this in your mind, think back to the days when social security was funded on a sound basis before extra benefits were added that were not prepaid by taxes. Now think of social security as it exists today with all the shortfall requiring current taxes to go out almost directly to recipients.

It makes sound, common business sense, therefore, to fund the liability when it is the smallest so that it is there when it is needed and when it is the greatest. Since something has to be paid sometime, I put the promise right in front of the corporation, right now when it is the smallest and the funding period is the longest, and it can be funded by any variety of investments. Life insurance makes the most sense because it takes all the burden away from the corporation in the event of death, and in the event of normal expectancy, through the use of the cash value. In this proposal, I was showing $250,000 of whole life and the premium was $455 per month. I was not suggesting the client pay monthly, but by illustrating it this way I demonstrated two effects. One, it shows that something has to be paid. Two, the figure of $455 per month looks miniscule next to $25,000 for 10 years. The implication here is that the cost of the promise is not a big one. The policy can be paid in any fashion, just like any other policy; very few pay it monthly, but it sure looks affordable when it is shown in this fashion.

The executive makes the three promises you see here. These are not hard ones to make if you intend to stay with the employer. They are especially easy if you are both the employer and the employee for whom the deferred compensation is being initiated. These three conditions are the ones that the IRS requires as the cornerstone to establishing this kind of a plan for an employee. Incidentally, the employee and the executive for whom I prepared illustration 24 are the same people. There was no distinction, but it makes some people feel important to hear themselves referred to as an "executive." It's one of those words that sells.

Under the section called, "Rights of Parties," I point out that the cash values are under the control of the company, by telling them that they may use the money they have put aside in the sinking fund. I chose the phrase, "Sinking Fund," for this proposal because I have so often heard this "sinking fund" used as an objection to life insurance. Now I take the word away from the side of objection and put it in the positive. The truth of the matter is: What does any of this have to do with insurance? We are talking about shifting a quarter million dollars to another segment of a person's life. Does it make any difference what the vehicle is called? It's the end result that matters and that is stated in the promises. If the word "insurance" by itself is strong enough to stop a financial arrangement, something is wrong with the presentation in establishing the need.

Point 2 under the rights is an interesting one. I tell the people that under no circumstances can the corporation ever be out more than $5,243. At this stage I will sometimes hear the question, "Do you mean we only pay three years and that's all?" I respond, "No, you will pay as long as the contract is in force or until age 65 whichever is shorter, but the contract develops its own equity and it has to be accounted for in some fashion. Therefore, it will be carried on your corporate books as an asset. By the second year, you will have paid a total of approximately $10,000. The plan has already begun developing its equity, which will be about $5,000. Therefore, in this second year, if you should quit the agreement and stop the funding, you will be out $5,243. After that this cost factor will diminish because the corporate asset will grow and the net cost will shrink."

If you have not spotted it already, this is the spot in the net cost column from the computer illustration that is the highest. I merely run my eyes down the column until I find the point where it bottoms out before it starts up again, and I plug this figure into the proposal. Obviously, it is different for each plan just as the amount of insurance and premiums are different. I do find, though, that I have hit upon a strong chord here by telling them the highest cost before they start objecting to the high cost of a plan.

The "Obligations of the Parties" are not tough. For the one side, it is a matter of keeping it current and for the other there is no change from the present, just as there is none under the "Rights of Parties."

This simple illustration seems to be a hit with the clients and their professionals. I have all the back-up paper for whoever wants to see it, but it rarely is needed. Most times the executives are happy to have a short, understandable meeting. Why muddle it up with too much? Some people, when asked what time it is, proceed to tell the questioner how the watch was made. We have this proposal on our word processor and it takes just a few short minutes to change any variables that have to be done. The only variables are the premium, the benefit and period, and the highest point of net cost.

When Congress goes to work, or when the IRS makes new regulations or rulings, we ought to send them thank-you notes instead of bemoaning our lot. Of course, it's a big job to conform to the changes they mandate, and customers are a little upset when we are the ones bringing them news of lesser benefits or higher costs either in premiums or legal fees. But if we do the work we are supposed to, our production can do nothing but go up. For the all-time example, let us think back to the "Big One." Social security was going to put us out of business. Think of it; before the Act, there was no social security. I know that it has now become so much a part of our culture that it is hard to imagine a time when there was none. But if some of the doomsayers are right, we will have no social security in the future.

Illustration 25. Flowery Estate Taxes

$500,000 JOINT LIFE- (ITF)
FLOWER BOND-ESTATE TAXES

| | | TONY   - 52 |
| | | MARILYN - 49 |

Year	Discounted Contribution	Redeemable Equity
1	$ 8,685	$ 0
2	8,685	10,196
3	8,685	20,198
4	8,685	30,690
5	8,865	42,225
	43,425	42,225
6	8,685	54,366
7	8,865	67,667
8	8,865	81,689
9	8,865	96,496
10	2,097	105,535
	80,262	105,535
11	0	112,662
12	0	120,006
13	0	127,607
14	0	135,992
15	0	144,708
	80,262	144,708
16	0	155,147
17	0	165,716
18	0	176,735
19	0	188,235
20	0	200,247
	$80,262	$200,247

JUNE 1983

This Saturday, when you're doing your clearest thinking, try to visualize that the voodooists are right and there will be no government payments to families for the early death, disability, or retirement of a worker. It's hard to get social security out of your thoughts because it is there, just like the mountains people climb. If you can think of a time in the future devoid of social security, then you have reached the state of our welfare posture prior to 1935. When the Act hit, it was going to be the end of us. The rest is history. We were all wrong, it only opened up the floodgates for insurance production undreamed of by anyone. I, for a lonely one, think there will always be social security. I cannot see it going out of existence. How we get taxed for it is the real question. The taxes can do nothing but get worse, but that too will neither eliminate nor bankrupt the system.

The point of the above is that every time the government makes a move, we benefit. We should be cheering them on, and instead of writing letters of protest or attempting to influence legislation for what we feel is in the best interests of the public, we should send them personal endorsements. We obviously care about the cost so we get involved in those projects we feel are not right. Maybe, just maybe, we're going about it in the wrong way. I developed illustration 25 to take advantage of the thinking in two of the government's recent moves. One was the elimination of "Flower Bonds." The other was the unlimited marital deduction.

The flower bond concept was one whereby a person could purchase a certain series of government bonds at the prevailing discount rate and hold them as an investment to maturity. If the individual died while still holding bonds that had not yet matured, they could be used in the payment of the estate tax. The benefit was that the bonds would be taken at face value even if at the moment prior to death they were worth something less. This was a tangible benefit and a great little extra incentive to get people to buy government bonds. Prospects would use this as an answer to objections, saying they could buy flower bonds to pay the estate taxes. It gen-

uinely was a bonus for those who did take advantage. It did
not cover all the estate tax needs for most decedents, but it
was always a good thing for them to talk about. The kicker
was the fact that few people did it; I only remember two of
my clients who owned some. But prospects liked to talk
about them to let us know there were other insurance-type
methods available without going to the insurance companies.
They also let us know they did their homework and read financial papers or had other financial planning outlets.

The benefit itself was a diminishing return since the difference between the present value and the maturity value
went down with time as the maturity date came closer. But I
must admit, the public was enthralled with the concept. Many
insurance sales were made on a flower bond type of interview
by building up this sudden maturity feature then explaining
that the discount was only 30 to 40 percent at the very start of
the period and diminished from there on. This was because
the original price of a $1,000 bond might be $600 or $700.
From there on it would grow closer and closer to the face
amount as time went by. The insurance analogy was easy to
do by comparing this cost of, say, 60 percent to a life premium of, say, 2 to 3 percent. The complement to this was the
discount of 30 or 40 percent for the bonds, to a 98 percent
scaling down for the life insurance. There was always a discount with the insurance while the bond would one day lose
its discount aspect.

The unlimited marital deduction was a part of the
Economic Recovery Tax Act (ERTA) passed by Congress in
1981. This gave married couples the greatest estate tax benefit
that could be had. The law changes all the time, but for now,
the first of a married couple to die passes the entire estate to
the other without taxes. It could be a puny estate or it could
be gigantic; it makes no difference. As long as the estate is set
up to pass to a surviving spouse, it goes over without stopping
for a tax bite. What this has done, to a minor degree, is allow
estate owners to hedge the funding and planning process by

counting on dying first, still married, and still having the estate.

This illustration works exceedingly well for persons who will ultimately, on the second death, have the big tax slug. I establish the need in the interview by telling the couple that there is no urgent estate tax need for insurance on the first death between the two of them. I explain the flower bond concept and bemoan the fact that it was taken away from us. I praise the present state of the tax laws that allow this huge allowance to be passed. I then do the math on what the taxes will be on the second death. I verbalize what a great chunk of money that will take and I ask, if the problem came up today, which assets they would sell to pay the bill. Would it be the house? The vacant land being held for development? The corporate bonds (which do not have the flowering attribute)? The stocks? The stamp collection? Or whatever personal asset they have that someone, someday, will decide is appropriate to sell just because of taxes. With this last line, I refer to taxes as "Welfare and Warfare Costs." It gets them angry to think where their money will be going.

I continue by saying, "The $500,000 in estate taxes does have to be paid; there is no avoiding it. But even that can be discounted. It can be brought down to the point where you only have to pay $80,262. How do you like that? It sounds good, doesn't it? But the insurance companies have gone to work and developed this product to such an extent that you don't even have to pay the whole $80,262 in one piece like you would in buying the old flower bonds. You can pay for it in 10 installments at the rate of $8,685 for nine years and $2,097 for the last year. At the end of 10 years, you have put in the entire $80,262 and the value of the asset has grown to $105,535. It continues to grow at about 6.5 percent forever after that until the death of both of you, and then the money is paid to your heirs so that the *cash* is there to pay the taxes. The family can then keep everything you have worked for and accumulated. It stays where it belongs and that is with the people you name to have it and not some anonymous

federal program. There is one major consideration and that is
the fact that this type of investment is so potentially profitable to the buyers that the insurance company has to have at
least a reasonable chance of getting the full $80,262; there-
fore, both of you must be able to pass a medical examination
to invest in it. Do you think you could do that?''

You have read just about the whole interview. That is
almost entirely what I say subject to some changes depending
on the conversation of the particular interview. You may not
recognize what illustration 25 developed from. It is a
Reader's Digest version of a second-death, joint-life policy,
with the dividends used pursuant to the "disappearing premium" concept. The ledger statement started out at the usual 12
or 13 columns. I boiled them down to the two that are shown
in the illustration. Since I was using a "flower bond" discounted concept, I called the premium "Discounted Contribution." The column called "Redeemable Equity" is the
cash value.

Notice at the top, I have put the letters, ITF. You will
recall this means "income tax free." I felt this was especially
important on this interview since we were talking about one
kind of tax. What a great place this was to have someone
question me about what the letters meant. On this particular
interview, they did not ask me the question so I explained it
myself as another feature.

I have shown that the object is to plant a word, phrase,
thought, inclination, or analogy in the client's mind. The purpose is to make a sale by talking about what is appropriate to
this interview and not straying too far or allowing old built-in
prejudices or misconceptions to creep in, to the extent they
destroy or detract from what is important. In preparing these
agendas and emaciated proposals, I have found that many
times the toughest part of a project is getting started. I can sit
for the longest time and stare at a blank page, but the minute
I write down the first word, I'm almost done. I may add to
what I've written or outlined. I may change its location on the

page, or I may simply scratch it out, but once I've started, I'm committed and, therefore, to my mind, almost finished.

The most important things are the words. There are words that control thoughts or actions without the listener ever knowing what is transpiring. I will give you some examples of mind-controlling words used in the stingiest, economical fashion, some of them of only one syllable. First off, let's take a look at the electronic opiate and Madison Avenue's greatest open forum: the television set (but not to forget the radio, newspaper, billboard, home-delivered flyer, and so on). The all-time best advertising slogan is, "New and Improved." Somewhere in a park on Madison Avenue, there should be constructed a statue honoring the genius who first originated that line. It was new and improved when he first brought it out. It is old and shopworn now, but it still works. We have heard it so much, we don't even hear it anymore. We don't even pay attention to it, but it is all around us. We see it, hear it, breathe it, assimilate it, taste it, and accede to it. It is impossible to be awake and not sense that trite expression and all the little stories, mysteries, situations, and vignettes that go with it. It's so bad and so repetitive, that it's good and fresh. Most times when we hear it on television, we swear to ourselves and promise not to listen, but when Suzie Gumchewer says, "New and Improved," our curiosity gets the better of us and we tune in to hear what silly hokum they're trying to dump on us this time. Then they've got us; they win again. The whole thrust of advertising is to get an audience. And the phrase just happens to work. Three little words, and they open up the receptacle.

Another advertising ploy is to use opposite phrases, or ones which bring back pleasant memories. Advertising, it could be said, is the purest form of selling. It is out-and-out basic cold calls and mass mailings. The idea is to get the message out to as many potential prospects as possible. There are objections, but the worst they can do is throw away the paper or shut off the night light. Either the customer buys the idea or not. There is no need for dialogue. The goal is to find the fewest, rightest words in the time allotted. A minute on a spectacular TV show can cost as high as a quarter-million dollars. One of the objects is to make the listener his own salesperson. We all know that a person does what he or she wants. If they feel they're being sold, they bring out the defenses; if they feel it is purely their own brainstorm, they buy. The technique is to start that storm in that brain. Really then, it is not unusual for the same product to be hawked for a long while as "New and Improved," then in a completely different ad campaign, to be presented as "Old-Fashioned," with all the "Down Home," "Good Old Days" thoughts that brings to mind.

Now think of the second all-time winner: "Free." We all know the counter to that: "There ain't no such thing as a free lunch." And for that matter, a free anything else, but let the word hit the ozone, and either positively or negatively, even by satellite or cable, the radar screen is set in motion and a listener is born and communication is in process. The rest of the message will be heard, consciously or not.

I can think of another one-word speech that is the major sales campaign of anyone under the age of 24. Try to get a teenager to do something by exhibiting all the patience, skill, charm, conviction, and knowledge you possess. The more you say, the more you invite resistance and the opposite action. But think back to your days of yesteryear or eavesdrop on the conversation of a bunch of kids, and hear the sales motto of the young set: "Chicken." Now we aren't talking about Kentucky-fried or pan-fried; I frankly don't know how it works. However, say "chicken" to a high-schooler and get out of the way; something is about to happen.

Some further examples of one-word messages that can elicit a lifetime of thinking follow. I will only mention a few of these words and I think my point will be made. Each of us in his or her own way will envision a total picture after just reading the words. Remember, they are just one-word catch-words designed to relate a total story. Consider what the shout of these words is trying to accomplish when they are ex-horted. The speaker is trying to report the calamity and at the same time, garner assistance. Maybe you have been present when these words were necessary. If so, you have experienced the result; if not, you can still appreciate the tension. Try these words out for effective communication: Fire!; Fight!; Rape!; Help!; and, Police!

Thinking back to the advertising business, who can resist the temptation of "Trial Offer," "No Money Down," or "Money Back Guarantee." The last is a surefire money-maker. So few people ever take the time to pack up something and send it back that the "Not Taken" ratio of this mass issue is very small. Think also of some of the shortest messages that denote a major event and get everyone's minds in gear. Try to recall all of the activity that takes place when a train conductor says, "All aboard." Most conductors even shorten the conversation to less than one word. When the conductor says, "'Board," it's final; there is no arguing. Either agree with him and do it his way, or don't go anywhere.

When your clock rings in the morning, you know exactly what that means. The message is out; the clock won't argue with you. A tremendous amount of debate and rationalization can go on in your head. The covers may be too heavy to lift, but the clock doesn't care. It has done its work in stimulating your brain to react.

That is my goal too.

What I attempt to do with the simplified illustrations and phrases, is immediately inject adrenalin and stimulation into the thought processes of the listener.

We can look far and wide, and travel great distances, at great expense, and call them "seminars" but the story of life is everywhere.

For instance, the title, "Universal Life" is a particularly appropriate one. Whether or not you believe in the product, or whether or not you sell the product does not make any difference; it does grab attention when one hears the phrase "Universal Life." It brings to mind, immediately, something that is all-encompassing, and something that we should—by nature—know about. We are expectantly waiting for the explanations so that everything starts falling into place.

*   *   *

9.

"YOU STILL IN THE INSURANCE BUSINESS?"

I'm sure you have heard that galling question: "You still in the insurance business?" I must admit that in recent years I have not heard it as much as I did when I was younger. But it used to drive me nuts to hear someone ask that question with an evil tone of expectancy in his or her voice, almost hoping that you will say, "No." Some people wish for the failures of others. I don't know if this is actually a real wish or just a cover-up for the fact that they feel a great deal of respect for the insurance agent and are harboring jealousy. A lot of agents are not successful, but I would not call them failures. This isn't an easy calling. I am not convinced that our turnover rate is any worse than any other profession, but when an agent is gone he is missed, and during the short tenures of some, they work hard and are visible.

Consider one of the noblest of professions, medicine, and measure the number of people who wash out of medical schools before they get those coveted initials after their names. Think about the number of athletes in the country who play college sports, and the small number who make it to the professional level. Think back even further and consider those who try for their athletic stardom without going to college but who go through all the sandlot and other semipro leagues. Is the turnover rate any better in the real estate industry?

It's lonely at the top and getting there is a long and tortuous road. One of the pitfalls of our business is the constant striving for excellence without even knowing when we have arrived. The new challenges and goals are astronomical. If the real measure of success were production alone, there would always be someone with numbers a little higher. It's a tough job and there are dropouts, but no one should be ashamed for having tried to measure up to the best he or she could do with what they have and then not being able to make a satisfying mark for themselves. In this business, we keep score with dollars of volume, income, taxes, expenses, conventions, plaques, and so on. Maybe we put the emphasis in the wrong place; maybe instead of just talking about millions sold, we should talk about millions created for families and retirees and be proud of the quality of work done rather than the dollar amount.

When I am asked today, after 28 years in the business, if I am still in it, I have the confidence and nonchalance to ask of the asker if they are still in their chosen work. I do it without malice or entrapment because it is an absolutely fair question. I find when they ask this question and I respond in kind, that the answer is often that the questioner has changed his or her occupation a number of times. We demand a lot of ourselves and perhaps that accounts for some of the dropout rate. But we should never be ashamed of striving for the best. However, in this arena of everlasting competition, we must take a little time for relaxation, so I throw in a few anecdotes about our clientele and about us.

We meet all kinds of people in our constant search for additional prospects. Some of the toughest to meet eventually become the closest of friends and clients. We might have a little reluctance about approaching someone, but a couple of years later when they are reluctant to call us asking for a favor or some extra service, we wonder why we had this fear of the initial call. They're as human as we are and if we have our little foibles, so do they. I think back to the day when I approached a personal client about getting a meeting with his senior partner who was older than both the client and me and much wealthier. He was a man who was held in awe and fearful respect by all of his associates. He was not a very personable man and even a little selfish.

He was tough on both my friend, Arnie, and me when we went to his office to talk about stock-redemption planning. He took a very narrow viewpoint and indicated the stores did not need this kind of protection; somehow they would take care of the families after death, and besides it cost too much. Nothing new in that argument and it is most generally a starting point for a sale, as it was in this case. He was looking at the problem from his own defined view because he had other interests and felt the value of this store was a small part of his total estate. I don't really know if he was right, but it is generally agreed that he is a very wealthy man. He was well-known about town and the frequent companion of political figures and sports celebrities. He was generous and lavish in his own lifestyle, but parsimonious with his associates and the kind of planning they desired. Truthfully, he was not a nice man to do business with. There was no doubt about his acumen, but his style was ruthless.

In any event, after a number of attempts, I placed a moderate amount of buy-sell insurance in one store and through the years did a lot of business with other acquaintances of this hard-nosed man. He respected me because of my standing up to him and my attitude of not caring whether he did business with me or not. We got along but it was a kind of armed truce. He was a difficult person to get close to and with whom to feel comfortable. This was a universally held opinion, and not just my own. His associates were all back-room lawyers about his methods when he wasn't around but yielded to him when he was present. He was tough, always got his way, and came out on top in every deal he ever made. His associates were unhappy with his demeanor but they liked the fact that he made money for all of them. He dominated these people.

Times got rough in their industry in 1980 and 1981. He was almost 60 and decided he did not want to go through the period of recession and rebuilding he was facing. He came to my friend with a proposition for selling the business. My friend really wanted the operation and was anxious to make a deal. The terms were no surprise to me, but they shocked my friend. He thought the business was worth much less because of the depressed retail conditions in Detroit at that time. The negotiations were tough and the tougher man prevailed with some onerous terms regarding every single asset the plan had. The younger one yielded on every point because he wanted the senior man out and at the same time had a youthful out-look on how to bring the business back to the good old days. Items he thought had no value were bargained away at top dollar. The cash of the business was drained off as a downpayment for the purchase. The business was really ravaged when the younger man finally got it. Nothing was forgotten and it was a shrewd piece of destructive bargaining for the older man.

After a few days, I got a phone call from the survivor, Arnie, telling me the story I just related. He asked me about the cash value of the policies that were in the corporation both on his life and the life of the former shareholder. I asked him if they had been a subject of discussion at the time of the buyout. He said they weren't since he and the other man had forgotten about them altogether. I told him there was a total value of $30,000 in all the policies on both lives. He asked what his options were.

He surrendered the policies on his former shareholder and borrowed all the money out of his. Happily, times have turned a little for him and the store is recovering. He freely admits that the insurance money was a saving grace. He still laughs about the fact that the former owner, who was the shrewdest negotiator he had ever known, allowed the deal to be sweeter for the victim than for the victor. I am also amused by the incident and have the feeling that the complete disdain of this man for insurance put a mental block in his mind about the subject, so that at the moment of most value for him, he never even thought of the policies that were corporate assets just like the goods in the warehouse. All his life he tried so hard not to think about insurance that at the most profitable moment, he got his wish and didn't think about it.

Throughout the book, you have seen my constant attempts to simplify and to eliminate paper. Let me tell you a story about a client who was the beneficiary of the bureaucracy's attempt to simplify matters by eliminating paperwork. Roger was a shareholder in a corporation that owned a chain of garment stores. He came to my office when he sold out to the other shareholders so that we could do the proper assigning of policies on withdrawal from the company. We completed our paperwork and were discussing what he was going to do with the cash from the sale of his stock. For his situation, annuities were the best answer. As I filled out the application, he asked me what birthdate I was putting down. I told him I was copying the one we used on all the insurance applications. He said that was okay, but his concern was evident. I asked him why he was inquisitive about this point and he told me the following story.

He came to this country as an immigrant in 1939. He was drafted to serve in the Army in 1942. At that time, he couldn't speak his new country's language very well, but he was defending that country in combat. An edict was issued stating that those who were not citizens but who served in the military could attain citizenship without the usual waiting period and testing. This was an authentic benefit of being in the service. He appeared for the ceremonies, which were completely perfunctory, and he did everything he was supposed to do, including filling out papers galore.

When he came to this country, he didn't speak a word of English. He was herded through checkpoints and, as best he could, he followed instructions, but he did not know what he was doing. Apparently, when the clerk filled out his application for entry, there was a mistake made in recording the date of his birth. He was made one year older than he really was. During the ensuing years, he had no need to look at the papers he had, nor could he fully understand them.

Now, on the occasion of his becoming a citizen, it was important to him that everything be right. Not only that, he could now read and understand the language. He noticed this error in his age and went to the captain in charge. It was important to him that all was exact, since he honestly appreciated this opportunity that had befallen him. He noticed the wrong birthdate and wanted it right. The captain told him, "Soldier, leave well enough alone. Don't make waves. It is a good thing for you. You will get your pension earlier than you should have. Besides, do you know how much work it is to correct all these papers? The paperwork is terrible. Just take it from me and you will be better off."

He did. And he is. His thought then, as a rookie GI, was to do as the ranking authority figures said; otherwise, there would have been big trouble. So, he left his birthdate as it was: wrong, and it came out that way on the citizenship papers he got and ultimately on the military discharge papers he received. Who could doubt such distinguished, official documents? From that time on, he was a year older.

He started working in a furniture store which he ultimately bought and made into a big and profitable business. Upon the ultimate sale of his business, he had no gainful employment. But in only one year after that he was eligible for social security. He now spoke the language very well and was savvy to the ways of the world. He figured that if he attempted to straighten out the mess at this point, he would be fighting a losing battle. So he applied for social security a year early and got it. Forty years ago, someone did not have to do his or her work and the cover-up did no harm until he reached retirement age and then it cost $800 per month for an extra year. Everything in life has a cost and this one was $9,600 to the other taxpayers. Who won this skirmish? I don't know. Will it ever change? I don't know. Carry, on, Oh Ship of State!

I have another story about a policyholder who didn't want to put all his eggs in one basket and then after paying the price of his own judgment, felt the insurance industry had let him down. I was only in the business a short while when I was given two cards for an "orphan" policyholder who had called in and asked for an agent to call. He was about to retire at age 65. I was elated when I saw the name on the card since the man was a former principal of one of the schools I had attended. I knew and respected him, and I was anxious to see him again and have him know how well I was doing in the insurance business.

He had two $12,500 policies with the company I represented. One was a participating policy and one wasn't. This was the time before we had computers plugged into the home offices and a time when the ratebook was a readable thing and the home office mail was an important happening. I determined his values and awaited the verification from the head office, since I did not want to make any mistakes on anything as important as the final play of the insurance cycle now that the policies would probably be either surrendered or placed on a paid-up basis. I also wanted to favorably serve my former principal. Each policy had a cash value of about $6,000. In addition, the par policy had dividend values of $6,000. I wondered why he had one of each, both applied for on the same day, but I thought I would get the answer to that during the interview.

When I met with Mr. S., he told me he had similar policies with two other companies. One was nonpar and one was par. He explained that one day in 1935, he had agreed with an "insurance broker" that he needed $50,000 coverage. The agent had promoted his company, which was participating, and had made the sale, which was very large for those days. Those definitely were not the days of million-dollar policies at travel accident rates. Because of the large size of the purchase, the client had talked to a number of people whose opinions he respected. He had heard the stories about the dividends not being guaranteed and the par policy being more expensive in the long run. He had also heard about the par company's policies possibly having a higher ultimate surrender value because of the dividend payments.

He came away from his research fully confused. After due deliberation, he decided to instruct his agent to apply for four policies, each for $12,500. Two would be nonpar and two would be dividend bearing. The two that I now represented were purchased from the same company, which at the time of issue had had both series. The others were with separate companies, one par, one nonpar. He already had the value statements from the other two companies and he said he was going to write back to the one because they had "forgotten to include my dividends."

I explained to him that I now had the same message for him regarding these two instant contracts. I also restated the differing philosophies of par and nonpar. He told me, "That's ridiculous. You're wrong." The cash values on all the policies were about the same; all in the range of $6,000. The dividends on the two par policies were pretty far apart. The two companies did have different experience but the important thing was, there were dividends and these policies were enhanced. He fumed awhile and asked me, "Why would anyone do such a thing?"

After I explained the differing philosophies of the two types of policies and offered what I thought had been his reasoning 25 years earlier, he started to recall some of his thinking at that time. It became clearer and he stated, "I didn't want to put all my eggs in one basket. I didn't trust any one of those companies any more than the other. I also couldn't really figure out the worth or nonworth of dividends so I made my decision to buy some of each. I wish I had purchased all of my insurance with 'N—M— Co.' It looks like I lost $12,000 of dividends." I told him he had the use of the money for the first few years until the policies started earning sufficient dividends to get below the nonpar. He said he didn't save that much money otherwise, and he didn't earmark any that was an offset from one kind of insurance or the other. So he did not have the "use of money."

He told me he was going to write to the nonpar companies and see if there was something they could do. I told him to save the energy. He already had their policies, which were fulfilled as promised, and he had their home office calculations, which officially informed him of their values. He wasn't happy but he understood.

In this book, I take no sides for or against one type of contract or another. I have heard and seen all the propositions and time value of money charts. I only relate what happened in this one incident. The moral of the story is that no matter what happens, if it is good, it was the person's own judgment and if it was bad, it falls upon the agent or the company. This particular man really did not have as great a problem as I can envision and have actually seen in other circumstances. Consider those individuals who buy term with the idea of investing the difference. I assume there might be those who do, but consider the degree of respect or disdain the agent who promotes this will bring upon himself or herself if the contract goes to retirement age when the policyholder may want to stop paying premiums during life. In most cases, the logic of buying term and investing the difference makes about as much sense as giving up smoking "to save the money."

When the question, "You still in the insurance business?" comes up, think about the spectacular experiences we would miss if we weren't in the insurance business. There are stories connected with every business, I'm sure, but the incidents that befall insurance people seem to have a particularly extraordinary impact. Maybe it's the fact that we work in somewhat of an adversary atmosphere, but when we get together with each other, the stories are unique. This next little incident I will relay could have happened anywhere in any business, but it was particularly geared to our business, which relies so much on prospecting for clients.

The search for new people is the most important activity in which we engage. This is true for the sales force and just as true for the management corps. When I first came into the business, our offices were in downtown Detroit. We were on the ninth floor of a large office building. Our agency was strictly a slice out of the mold of the typical insurance agency of the 1950s and 1960s; all the agents were housed in the office and there was not too much brokerage going on, either from the inside going out or the outside coming in. We were strictly a homogeneous group of primarily young guys with a strong, purist manager. The late Mr. A.G. Billesdon was a manager in the truest sense. When he became manager he gave up selling, so the thought of sales for commissions left his mind. He competed with his agents in neither time nor prospects. His job, of course, was to make young people successful and he was a marvel at doing it.

On the same floor, there was a very successful casualty agency. In those days, there was not a lot of crossover of life with property and casualty. They didn't seem to mix too well, or at least the people did not allow it to mix too well. It was a situation of "never the twain shall meet." In keeping with the general theme of the times, neither did the personnel meet. I didn't know anyone from the other agency and I don't think anyone else did. I know for certain that Mr. Billesdon didn't. If we were to take a little time to reflect, each of us could come up with some pretty humorous memories of how we met different people in our lives. I don't think any could be as humorous as how Mr. Billesdon met the head of this P&C agency and recruited one of the most outstanding brokers the agency ever had.

One day, the two of them were standing together doing nature's business in the men's bathroom. As casually as two people can be at that moment, they said, "Hello" and "How's business?" They used the two washbowls together and Mr. Billesdon asked the other man if they did any life business. The answer was negative and from that soggy start, there developed a lifelong personal friendship and a mutually profitable business relationship. This only proved that our manager practiced what he preached: the prospects are everywhere; you only have to ask.

That was a funny incident, but let me now relate one that illustrates some of the things we point out to our business clients when we first start talking to them. We tell them of the instant difference between a wife and a widow. We tell them of the changes in goals and needs of the survivors and heirs that take place when death occurs. Too often they are taken as stories told by the agent just to stimulate a desire. For sure, there is some of that in our needs exploration, but the stories are all true. This particular business was a partnership between Jim and Eric, each owning 50 percent of a retail electrical appliance store specializing in lamps.

I came to the case on a referral basis from another client. I was not made fully welcome when we started to talk. Eric was the majordomo of the two of them and Jim had little to say. He saw me out of respect for the referrer and out of a little bit of curiosity bordering on nosiness. I think he wanted to know a little of the secret stuff of the other person's business. Before we really got going, Eric told me this visit would be nonproductive, but I could talk if I wanted to. The exact words were, "We are friends and have been partners for over 18 years. We have a good agreement and we know what we want to do if one of us dies. We're not buying any insurance, but we'll listen.'' With this not unfamiliar, chilling invitation to help these people, I started an interview.

Since he mentioned they had a buy-sell agreement, this seemed like a good place to start. Frankly, after the chastising tone, I would have been quite happy to leave the premises without even going any further. Then, one of the obligations to the center of influence came into being. No matter what I thought of these people, my referrer saw them in a different light and I can't violate that trust. So my attitude had to be completely solicitous for the well-being of this business on a thoroughly objective basis, although subjectively, I had other emotions only a few words away. I felt I wanted to get reorganized for this case, so I asked if I could see the agreement or take it with me. Eric said I could see it right there, but it wasn't going to leave the store. Then came a funny part that all of you have seen over and over again: looking for papers or documents that haven't been seen for years. It was like a scene out of an old-time slapstick movie to watch the two of them flitting around from file to file and desk to desk and to the office in front trying to find their partnership file. It was taking so long and making them so frustrated that I offered to come back or have them mail it to me. Their attitude changed during this frantic search. I think they started to think about the mortality of people and businesses when they could not find the evidence of there even being a business. In fact, they now became a little more caring of my time and asking me to please bear with them for just a little longer.

Voila! When the office looked sufficiently like burglars had been there, it turned up. Triumphantly, Jim said, ''There, we have it. Now you can see that everything is taken care of.'' I sat down on a couch and started to read the contract. It was uncomplicated and short. When I finished, I said, ''You are right. You have taken care of a very effective buyout. It is all spelled out for you and the funding is in place. But I'll make you a deal. I'll buy you out right now for twice the amount you will receive later on at death. I'll give each of you $40,000 for your halves.'' They were confused by my attitude and the seemingly silly offer. Eric said, ''What do you mean $40,000 for my part? The place is worth $200,000, easy.'' I responded, ''I don't doubt that but, on death, it is only worth $20,000 to each of you. It says so in the agreement. The price is fixed and there is no reopening clause for updating the price.''

With that they both lowered on me saying I was wrong. The $20,000 was the first price they agreed on for the initial value 18 years ago, but there is a clause saying the value is to be on a ''book'' basis at death. They told me the initial $20,000 policies were to be a downpayment if the business were worth more, and the balance would be paid out over a few years. I told them I could be wrong; why don't they look at the contract. Eric took it and sat down. He looked at Jim and said, ''He's right, but didn't we make another change with the lawyer?'' They couldn't agree so I suggested they call the lawyer right now. He was in his office but didn't have the time to get their file out immediately. He could not recall any changes to the original agreement, however.

Finally, we all agreed that although there may have been an intention to change and update this agreement, it was never done and what they still had was a stipulated value that was completely out of date. They both protested that they were friends and that the survivor would never hold the family of the deceased to that ''old thing.'' I interjected, ''Are you sure? I know you can speak for yourselves, but take a good look at your partner and try to figure out what he would really do when the moment of truth were at hand, and more importantly, where is he going to get the money to be a nice guy? Then consider all the cheap advice he is going to get from everyone—from the lawyer, banker, wife, cousin-in-law, and the boys at the lodge.''

The rest of the discussion was great. It was selling to two people who felt they had just awakened from a bad dream and could now get their feet back on solid ground. We set up two $80,000 policies and made arrangements to get the document touched up to reflect a book value buyout, which is what made them feel comfortable. They agreed that if the insurance were below the book value, it would act as a down-payment and the balance would be paid over 60 months. If the insurance were in excess of the book value, the total policy would be paid.

Business was not good for them in the late 1970s and a couple of premiums had gone on automatic premium loan. In 1980, Jim died and Eric called me. The total claim paid from the two policies was $94,000 after deduction for loans. I gave the checks to Eric, who said he did not know if he was going to continue the business because of his advanced age and the uncertainty of doing it without his lifelong partner. This was a rather touching meeting and I felt a lot different about him than I had the first time we had met and I wanted to get away from him.

But, he called me two days later and he was once again a different man. He explained that the last few years of business had not been so good and the book value was about $75,000 for Jim's interest and he did not know if it would be proper for him to pay $94,000 for the purchase. I told him I thought there was no choice since the agreement made it very clear about what the procedure would be. He didn't agree with me and started to read me the language over the phone. He was trying to slant the meaning of the buy-sell document. The crowning question was, "I wonder what Jim would have done to me?" I told him to call the lawyer and he would instruct him as I had.

He didn't call me back, and after two weeks I called him to see what had been done. He told me that he had paid the full $94,000, but did so reluctantly since there was some room for doubt about what the agreement's precise meaning was. In other words, the lawyer had told him to pay the full amount but he was still wheedling and trying to justify a selfish opinion.

It's amazing how frequently the hypothetical situations we pose to clients actually come to pass in time. I guess if we stay in this business long enough, Murphy's Law will come true in all facets of our operations. This case was a revelation to me about how cheap one man would try to be and I wonder what his reasoning would have been under the old agreement, which had the stipulated price of $20,000. The answer they gave me on the first day of our meeting was a pure lie. They said they would take care of each other. On the other hand, maybe it was not a lie, because "take care" can have more than one meaning.

*   *   *

10.

NEVER ON SUNDAY

Remember the popular song, "Never on Sunday"? It told about a girl who could be kissed any day of the week but Sunday. Her protest was, "That's my day of rest." She was right. We all need the day of rest. The theme of this book is relaxed selling, but I've taken you on a trip of hard work explaining some of the things I do in my work. I presented Saturday as a day of rest and work at the same time. Weekends may have been made for a popular kind of beer, but I think they serve a pretty good purpose in getting the body ready for the week that follows. For maximum performance on Monday, we'd better treat the body right over the weekend.

As I mentioned, I'm a sports fan and like to watch sports on TV Saturday afternoon. I think some of the most intelligent people I have ever seen are the top-notch athletes who are the best in their own fields. The smartest are the really young ones like track stars or swimming stars who are veterans by the time they are 18. It is astonishing to hear a 16-year-old kid, whose face still shows the signs of puberty, tell the announcer that he or she is planning to have a great summer, then relax for a few months while preparing mentally for the indoor season, and time his or her training program so the peak is at the big international meet. I have heard others explaining their training regimen and then talk just as enthusiastically about having a week off to themselves. I remember seeing one young lady who had just won an Olympic gold medal telling how she had celebrated her victory the night before. She was delighted that her parents had been with her for the victory; they had taken her to a massive dinner to fete the champ. Her relaxation was to allow herself a dessert for the first time in months. "What'd ya have?" asked the announcer. I'm sure he anticipated some gooey, fudgy, sugary concoction. Her answer came with childlike candor, but with the appreciation of an honestly deserved reward: "Vanilla ice cream."

The kid was completely at ease. She could stop her training and have nothing to do for a long time, if she chose. She didn't have a meet for two months. She could have said anything she wanted about the spoils of time off. Whatever she would have said would have been right. When she needed peak performance, she had all the winning elements. The purpose of this relaxation stage was to clear out all the cobwebs and psychological regimentation. This was down time. This was the time to do something completely out of character. This was the time to unwind. For her, it was a bit of vanilla ice cream.

Everybody and everything need some down time. Think about some things that run all the time and are expected to go on indefinitely. An air conditioner is one of these things. My office is in a building that has no windows that can be opened. Therefore, we are dependent on the heating and cooling system being functional all the time. We all know that is an impossibility; it breaks down on occasion. Some of these breakdowns could be prevented with more regular, planned shutdowns for service. Worn parts and equipment could be replaced when signs of wear and tear first appear. The system happens to work very well, but there are those days when the heater or cooler breaks down. Appropriately, it always seems those are the days when the weather is the most extreme and we can't live without our fresh air supply. When things are going well, we never pay attention to the items we take for granted.

One of the things we take for granted is our health. When things go well, we don't think about illness. We can bring it to mind, but it's tough to really experience the toothache if you don't have it right then. Most people are pretty sensible about their personal diet and exercise habits. There are those who have no control in either and the results are evident. If these things and others, like smoking, get out of balance, quick measures can be taken to bring them under check. We all know the steps but sometimes don't take preventative measures soon enough, which often requires us to take the remedial ones by force of necessity.

There is a life other than work and it too requires planning and some effort of its own. This is the down time I refer to and each of us must have some of it. I have friends and clients who say their work is their play and vice versa. One man said to me that work is what you *have* to do, relaxation is what you *want* to do. He thereby rationalized his boundless energy, which was all spent at his shop. His business was his narcotic and he fell into that category known as "workaholic." Some of us can do this forever without showing signs of wear, but most of us have to shut off the engine for just a little while at regular intervals. Sunday is a good day to do that because everybody feels the same way about it at the same time. Therefore, most business places are closed and the majority of the populace is at home, at rest.

But it doesn't have to be on Sunday; it could be at any time. Indeed, many people have different days off. Traditionally, doctors took off on Wednesdays. Tennis clubs are loaded and it's tough to get a court on that day. One of the nice parts of our business is the ability to make our own work schedules. We can work when and as much as we want. There is that old saying, "TGIF," meaning, "Thank God It's Friday." This is an anticipatory plaint about the coming weekend. It serves as a good mental lift to get the mind to higher achievements just by breaking the routine for a moment and thinking about the release of pressure.

The pressure is the villain. The constant grind with little relief can cause great bodily harm. We used to call it "stress," but it has come back to visit us in a new suit. In the jet age it is known as "burnout," or for a more advanced case, "executive burnout." It can happen to all of us and it can skip most. I contend that a person can do more work in eight hours a day than he or she can do in 12. I also think that he or she can do more in 11 months than can be accomplished in 12 months. We are blessed with a fine secretarial staff and we trust them all. When a secretary comes to me with a request for a day or afternoon off to take her child to the dentist or do some personal business, I say "yes" before the sentence is finished. I usually cut off the words in midstream because I want to say, "yes" before I hear the reason. It doesn't make any difference what the reason is. If a person does a good job and knows his or her responsibilities and can arrange the affairs of the station so that time off can be had, my answer will always be a rapid-fire, affirmative one. Think about the conflict that occurs when you must say "no." If the person disagrees with your call, he or she can be at the workplace but not fulfill the tasks that are required. The body is there but the mind is playing out the scene from Murphy called, "Work will expand to fit the time allotted."

I had a funny incident happen to me. A couple of years ago, I got myself into the state where I was listless and not feeling well. I had some physical symptoms and I went to see a doctor. After the standard, metered, cash-register tests sufficient to make it appear legitimate, he said I was suffering from fatigue. I decided to go to a psychologist for further consultation. I met with him for a few months. Early in the visits, he determined that I had "stress" and should learn to slow down. He really helped and I did slow down and felt better in a short time. He did teach me how to relax. This psychologist was a very interesting man. He only worked at his practice four-and-a-half days per week. In his spare time, he had formed a manufacturing firm with a couple of friends.

The business was going well and he started to change the mix of time between the practice and the corporate duties. During this period, I set up buy-sell and key-man insurance for his manufacturing business. Eventually, the business became very lucrative and he stopped seeing patients and went to work full time in the other business. He soon gained some weight, started smoking, and looked weary. Business was good but it was a different arena and the demands were not similar to the one-on-one world of helping people with thier own problems. This enterprise, fledgling that it was, encountered growing pains. Mind you, they were good pains and the firm was going forward, but the pressures of sales, deadlines, and payroll were now more imminent and exceedingly larger.

About six months after he went full time, I was in the office with him and one other shareholder. I had just come back from a nice trip, business was good, I was breezing at my work and relaxing as he had taught me to do. He commented that I was looking good. I thanked him and told him it was actual, and I was very happy with my new outlook. I was going to ask, but before I did, he said, rather plaintively, "I'm not doing so well. I haven't had time for racquetball for weeks, I've gained weight, I've started smoking again, and I feel low." I responded sincerely, "Do you want to talk?"

Life ain't easy in a pressure cooker, and that is what many of us make out of our daily affairs. Saturday always comes. It's a great day for me and it seems to be a great day for everyone. When I schedule an appointment for a Saturday, I always think in advance that the law of averages on this case are stacked in my favor. I think of what is going on here. The prospect has given me some of his most precious time, the time he could be using just for himself alone. He agreed to meet with me so it must be a subject he takes seriously. It is tough to hold a meeting on a normal day off, when there are a whole gang of other things one could be doing. The clients are relaxed on Saturdays, so the satellite dish in the brain is ready for clear reception. A Saturday case is a good one for another reason. With the good odds on your side, you will probably start Monday morning off on a high note because you are coming in with a signed application. The week seems more ripe for further sales when you are already on the scoreboard.

What one does on leisure time makes no difference, so long as the brain has a short vacation. One of the quickest fixes possible is reading and I don't mean heavy industry study material. Books like this one are fine; you're on the right track if you've gotten this far. Sports are great. I play a lot of racquetball, some of it at lunchtime. I once had someone ask me how I could do that and wasn't I exhausted for the rest of the day. The answer to that question is, "Absolutely not." I feel great after a workout and ready for new projects. The stimulation is both physical and mental. An hour of ball is like an hour nap.

Clubs and committees are valuable. Especially so, if you are not using them as just another prospecting tool. If you are in a charity that is worthwhile, just doing a good job for the organization will bring you business without looking for it. The members will seek you out as a good and competent adviser because of the good and competent duties you have performed for the group. People sense sincerity when there is no profit to be made, and they want you on their team when there is a profit to be earned. Honest effort never goes unrewarded.

Not seeing the forest for the trees is a common problem. It happens to all businesspeople. We must step back sometime and admire what we have done. If we don't, how do we know what we have done, or more importantly, when we are done? Even a robot wears out. Have you ever had an idea or a name escape your recall and no matter how hard you thought, it would not come to mind? Then, after you have given up in frustration and changed the pressure level, it suddenly pops into your mind. That is the subconscious. The knowledge was in there but the avenues out were clogged. Relaxing allowed the information to get out. For some of us this happens frequently when we give ourselves an overdose of education and seminars. So much information comes flowing, we are afraid of all that is behind it. We wonder about our own competence and start doubting some of the unique planning devices we have installed for our clients. This is not an unnatural phenomenon and when it happens maybe it is a small warning to step back and take off some pressure.

Making a living and building a career are not easy jobs. If it loses all the joy when it is being performed, is it worth it? I hope this book has caused you to realize there is an easier way to do the same tasks. For me the most pressure was in front of the clients. Sometimes I was thinking so hard that I wasn't really thinking at all. Preparing in advance has relieved most of that. Also, preparing agendas and illustrations that are recyclable has paved the way for less time on the interviews and more time off. The interviews are more effective and the other interests are too.

Next week when the pressure builds up, and the end is nowhere in sight, make an appointment with yourself along with all the others you rush to keep. Sit down and talk to yourself. Think about what I think is the greatest relaxation of all: time with your family. They need you too; otherwise, the gains may actually be losses. Time marches on and kids grow up. The young girls and boys that we marry become the middle-aged people that we see on our interviews every day. That happy couple that you interview is you at some other time and some other place. Share with your family what they need the most: *quality time.*

In conclusion, I say to you that Saturday always comes. As a dedication for this book, my blessing is that it always comes with Sharon.

*   *   *